Library of Congress Catalog Number: 2001018460
ISBN: 0-89503-257-0 (cloth)

Library of Congress Cataloging-in-Publication Data

Golubow, Mark, 1957-
    For the living : coping, caring, and communicating with the terminally ill / Mark Golubow.
        p. cm.
    Includes bibliographical references and index.
    ISBN 0-89503-257-0 (cloth)
    1. Terminally ill. 2. Terminally ill- -Care. 3. Terminal care. 4. Physicians- -Interviews.
    I. Title.

R726.8 .G65 2001
362.1'75- -dc21   2001018460

Table of Contents

SECTION ONE:
Oncology Healthcare Professionals

SECTION TWO:
A Symbolic Interactionist Look at
Death and Dying

Acknowledgments

I am indebted to many people for their support in writing *For The Living*.

Shirley Driks, Rich Ray, and Kelly Otter helped transcribe and edit many hundreds of recorded words over the last ten years, and my friend Amy Heffner assisted in editing the final manuscript. Paul Greenberg started the transcribing process by introducing me to both Shirley Driks and Rich Ray when I didn't know who could help transcribe my taped interviews. Thanks to them all.

I wish to recognize the assistance of several people in academia. I could not have completed this book without the benefit of the courses taught by Professors Linda Lederman, Hartmut Mokros, and Jennifer Mandelbaum of Rutgers University, as well as the many private exchanges of ideas. Most significantly, they helped me gain a better understanding of myself and the world around me. I also thank retired New York University Professor Carl Schmidt, mentor and friend during my last two years at NYU, for his unwavering confidence in me (and for our New York Yankees talks!). Professors' Deborah Borisoff and Joyce Hauser at NYU not only gave me my first opportunity to teach, but also supported me with their humor and practical advice inside and outside the classroom. My long talks with Professor Asli Gokhan-Kucuk at the Fashion Institute of Technology enabled me to become a better person and educator.

Thanks also go to Les Weinstock, Diane Behl, and Sam Klein, friends from the old Oncology Division at Ciba-Geigy, for their steadfast loyalty to this project from its earliest years. I will forever be grateful to my oncology manager, Gerald Reed, for his close friendship during the turbulent years of coping with my father's death and for teaching me what humanistic leadership is all about. Thanks to Howard Grossman for his help during this difficult time of my life, as well.

I wish to express my gratitude to long-time friends Arthur Garfinkle, Glenn Consor, Carolyn Saunders, and Rob and Janet Myers;

my brother-in-law Arthur Wagner, nieces Julie and Jennifer Wagner, my sister Robin Wagner, and my mother, who always seemed to be there when I needed them and to be concerned with my writing and my everyday life.

I have nothing but praise for the great people at Baywood Publishing—Bobbi Olszewski, Joi Tamber-Brooks, Julie Krempa, and Baywood president, Stuart Cohen—for their professionalism, patience, and kindness. I could not have completed this book without them. I'm also beholden to Dr. Jack Morgan, chief editor and guiding light of *For The Living,* for the foresight—and the faith in a first-time writer—to turn the idea for this book into reality.

Finally, I am indebted to all the oncology health care professionals, those who appear in this book and those who do not, such as Bernice Linderman, retired oncology nurse at Coney Island Hospital, who shared their thoughts and feelings with me. And I thank Dr. James Wernz, a man of remarkable dedication and compassion in his work and his relationships with patients, who gave me the idea to write a book on the experiences of oncology health care professionals.

Introduction

*Life helps us to shape our thoughts about death, and often
serves as our metaphor, the known invoked to adumbrate the as
yet inexperienced. Hence to talk at all interestingly about death
is inevitably to talk about life.*

                                                                    D. J. Enright

The longest distance (or shortest, depending on your outlook) between
birth and death is life. In his landmark work *The Denial of Death*, Ernest
Becker (1973) describes what he thinks life is like between these two
primal endpoints:

> I think that taking life seriously means something such as this: that
> whatever man does on this planet has to be done in the lived truth of
> the terror of creation, of the grotesque, of the rumble of panic
> underneath everything. Otherwise it is false. What ever is achieved
> must be achieved from within the subjective energies of creatures,
> without deadening, with the full exercise of passion, of vision, of
> pain, and of sorrow (pp. 283-284).

The implication of Becker's words is that during our life each of us
somehow finds our own path to death. A path that can only be lived on
with any truthful and passionate meaning by accepting the terrifying
notion that the prospect of dying shadows us everywhere we go. Such
thinking forces us to look seriously at who we want to be, where we are,
and where we're going in life regarding our self and relationships that
comprise our day-to-day social lives with family, friends, and work. In
many respects, then, the time we do have can teach us to view death, or
the fear of death, not so much as an enemy, but as a principle motivating
force behind human behavior.

A discussion along these lines on life, death, and mortality is not
easy. Our daily activities are largely constructed to evade, ignore, or
deny the prospect of dying. Consequently, even though the prospect of

1

death permeates our society, culture, and lives each day there remains a general reluctance against speaking about death. Seldom do we know what to say or do when someone is dying. And rarely do we use the experience of loss or caring for someone who is dying as a way of learning about ourselves, everyday relationships, and roles in society more deeply. As we will see, further insights into these social and cultural issues surrounding death and dying helps in understanding the complex meanings behind the behavior of the people that are represented in this book.

Between 1991 and 1993 I interviewed thirty oncology healthcare professionals, such as doctors, nurses, and social workers in order to find out what it was like for them to treat people who were dying. My feeling was—and still is—it is rare in our society that we seek out or listen to the thoughts, feelings, and behavior toward life, death, and dying from the perspective of the caregiver. And oncology professionals have a unique perspective on the process of dying being that they choose to work in that environment on a daily basis.

In this sense, the twelve narratives that appear in the accompanying chapters are more than about sickness and dying. They are personal experiential accounts of how working with dying patients impact the lives of a small group of oncology health professionals who routinely face mortality and loss everyday. My hope is that the experiences shared by these doctors, nurses, and social workers can provide caregivers with a resource to better understand their own experience with death and it's role in life, while helping others with terminal illness.

The influence of this book largely depends on how the narratives of the oncology healthcare professionals and associated theoretical concepts relate to the reader's own life experiences. There are likely to be readers who wish to read these personal stories without a theoretical interpretation and decide alone, with friends, or colleagues, what story is important to them. Others may look forward to a traditional analytical uncovering of meaning in order to gain deeper awareness into the behavior and work environment of the medical oncology professional, as well as their own. For these reasons *For The Living* has been organized in the following manner:

SECTION ONE:
ONCOLOGY HEALTHCARE PROFESSIONALS

Section One provides readers the opportunity to read the recorded narratives of twelve oncology healthcare professionals' without any interjection of formal analysis and discover on their own which ones are relevant to their everyday lives. There are two narratives from social workers, three from nurses, and seven from doctors. Due to the sensitive nature of subject matter, and promise of confidentiality, people's names and places of work have been changed.

Although there is no conventional analytical interpretation of events there are recurring communicative and behavioral themes associated with the doctors, nurses, and social workers that appear throughout each interview. Several of these topics and related acts are discussed in greater detail in Section Two.

SECTION TWO:
A SYMBOLIC INTERACTIONIST LOOK AT
DEATH AND DYING

This section takes an in-depth theoretical look into the possible reasoning and motivations behind oncology healthcare professional's actions in treating cancer patients.

Three prevalent death-related experiences are selected from the narratives of several oncology healthcare professionals and examined within the theoretical framework of symbolic interactionism. The three death-related experiences are called *Acts of the Self, Acts of Coping,* and *Acts of Communication.*

By integrating the death-related experiences of oncology healthcare professionals within the theoretical framework of symbolic interactionism readers can reflect on their experiences in a more comprehensive manner. Once this comparison is made readers can determine to completely apply, modify, or reject the narratives and/or theory's premise for practical use in their day-to-day world.

All cited work and interpretive analysis of events and behavior connected with the lives of the oncology healthcare professionals used in Section One and Section Two are based upon my current role and perspective as Ph.D. student and qualitative researcher in the field of communication at Rutgers University.

Prologue

The red light to the phone machine was blinking wildly. It was the 27th of September 1989, a Wednesday night. I pressed play. Robin, my sister, had left two messages, asking to call her as soon as I got these messages, for "It was important." She left the messages at 7:45 P.M. and nine o'clock. Marion, my stepmother, left a similar message around eight. It was now ten. Their tone was controlled, but urgent. I knew. I just knew. "He's dead, isn't he?" I asked my sister when she picked up the phone. She asked me how did I know. "I don't know, I just did," I replied unemotionally. My sister wanted me to come over and be with her. There was no one with her from the immediate family or close friends to offer emotional support. My mother had left earlier. My sister's husband, Artie, could do so much. Neither one of us felt close to Marion. She wanted me. But I did not want to drive to Queens. I told my sister I needed to be by myself and would come over tomorrow. She did not like this, and could not understand my thinking. "Didn't I need to be with someone?" A damn good question in retrospect, but at the time all I could muster was "Sure, but not tonight. I don't mean to be unkind, Rob, I just feel I need to be by myself. I can't explain it. I promise I will be there tomorrow, okay?" We hung up. I slid down to the floor of my apartment, back to the wall, legs out, hands on lap staring blankly through the window of my bedroom into the Brooklyn night. The phone rang. My body jumped. It was Smitty. He wanted to know how I was doing. I said I wasn't sure. I couldn't feel anything. I was numb. Nothing like this had ever happened to me. I asked him how he was doing. He said he was feeling a void. His best friend for forty years was no longer around. We reminisced about all the high school basketball games my dad and Smitty saw me play in. My father never missed a game—home or away—for three years. I reminded Smitty how my dad also saw many of my baseball and softball games right until I left home for college. I recalled how my dad and I never missed a James Bond opening at the Fresh Meadows movie-theater. Afterwards we always headed over to

5

Janes Restaurant on Queens Blvd. for a vanilla banana split. We talked more, more about how my dad was always there for us when we needed help. He was always there. Even if he disagreed with what you were doing, if it was important to you, he supported it. He would call after major events in my life to see how things turned out, a ball game, a job interview, a business meeting, whatever. He was always there. After an hour I thanked Smitty for calling. I went back to staring out into the night. Slowly it dawned on me. I never saw it, not once in thirty-two years; the unconditional love my father had for his friends, Robin, and me. I grabbed my knees and pulled myself into a ball on the floor, rocking back and forth. Feeling very alone, anchorless. Crying. I too had just lost the best friend I ever had.

Prior to my father's death I don't believe I was living a fulfilling life. Each day was routinely like the next with no significant conviction toward another person, work, or social cause. My role and place in life was undefined. Since then, everything I have done, wish to do, and become has been a direct or indirect result of coping with my father's death.

During the early 90s, my volunteer experiences with the American Cancer Society, helping people with HIV/AIDS, and interviews with oncology healthcare professionals enabled me to recognize personal issues of mortality, which I was unconsciously dealing with after my father died. That thought, that fear of dying, remains a constant motivating force behind many life choices, including writing this book, and getting a Ph.D. in the field of communications.

The relationships I've had over the last decade with mentors, healthcare professionals, and trusting friends at school and work encouraged me to continue on a journey of personal discovery that was at first scarily unsteady, but as time went on became more confident and solid. Thanks in large part to this faith others had in me I have found a desired and meaningful spot in life. The death of my father and subsequent relationships affected me in other ways as well.

I have often felt that I am a unique individual, in that I have the ability to create my own destiny, free of social and cultural constraints. This is not the case anymore. I still believe in freedom of choice, but I now understand that choices and identity can be limited if not assisted through the help of others and activities within socially constructed environments or communities, such as education, business, and volunteerism. This acknowledgment has been a radical one for me since I had always looked at life chiefly through an individualistic and psychological point of view.

If identities and lives are continually evolving and constructed in varied environments over time it stands to reason that any interpretive form of events or behavior is just one way in which to make sense of the world and one's place in it within an historical and present context.

By accepting this open-ended world view the structure of my life is now clearer. Deciding which communities to explore has been a curious and exciting challenge. My growth seems endless. I recognize that any limitations on personal growth will come from being uncomfortable or fearful of trying something new or exploring unknown environs.

But life is about change and adaptation. Change in one's life is a given, like death. And the death of a loved one, or a patient, can create many revisions in a person's world. How an individual deals with life changes brought on by death and the prospect of dying or, as Becker termed in the introduction "the rumble of panic underneath everything," can greatly shape his or her identity and daily behavior.

With this thought in mind, our attention shifts toward the recorded experiences of twelve oncology healthcare professionals who choose to face the rumble of panic underneath everything every day.

SECTION ONE

Oncology Healthcare Professionals

In environment where ugliness and disintegration file past one's eyes like a permanent movie, the provider sees him or herself unwillingly plunging into the vulnerability of corporal existence. One therefore experiences simultaneously the perverse effects of compassion and the cold evidence and flimsiness of one's own aesthetics.

Serge Marquis, M.D.

WHAT TO EXPECT

What can be expected by peering into the publicly closed community of oncology healthcare professionals?

Someone once said, "Every man has within himself the entire human condition." The inference being that whenever an individual openly talks about oneself, to some degree, that person is talking about all of us. This comment holds particular truth for the oncology healthcare professional, for at the heart of these twelve disparate narratives is a certain unity to human experience.

The behavioral and communicative acts surrounding death and dying are as complex for the oncology health professional as it is for anyone else. Oncology healthcare professionals, however, have a unique outlook on the process of dying being that they choose to work in that environment and see it every day. There are few, if any, individuals and occupations that fully view and exercise with such consistent intensity the human condition of passion, pain, and sorrow than oncology doctors, nurses, and social workers treating terminally ill patients.

What death and the prospect of dying therefore means to the individuals whose stories appear in this segment should not be taken lightly. Reading what others do, say, think, and feel is a beginning for readers to reflect on their own death-related experiences, which may lead to picking up new perceptions of death and ways of handling it in everyday interactions.

This section places the value of each story on life experience, rather than any academic interpretation of events. An in-depth theoretical analysis of the doctors', nurses', and social workers' thinking and behavior is provided in Section Two. Section Two will give readers added insights into the meanings and motivations behind the oncology healthcare professionals' actions, and possibly their own. Be that as it may, sometimes it is necessary to step back and simply let certain stories speak for themselves.

CHAPTER 1
Social Workers

CINDY

Getting the diagnosis of cancer is a bombshell. It's like an explosion. It's a tremendous explosion in a person's life. They don't have the time to process that because decisions need to be made right away. The diagnosis has to be made, and then, often surgery starts or chemotherapy will begin or combinations of things happen. The patients don't process the bombshell, they respond. They have to get as much information as they can. They choose health professionals. They start off on this whole treatment course. And they are busy dealing with that. It's like a real crisis stage, everyone is mobilized and energized, and "we're going to fight." The family rallies together. There is a sense of hope and optimism initially. You've got the best health professionals behind you, everyone is working as a team on your treatment. The doctors may by saying very positive things about the outcome. There is a kind of feeling of security that you are doing everything you can. The oncologists may have good results with the initial bout with cancer.

Then what happens is the treatment may become routine, and you get a sense that you are in it for the long term. After the initial recovery from surgery, chemo, or radiation, sometime down the road, the impact of the bombshell starts to set in. And often a difficult time is when treatment ends. First you're caught up in the energy and mobilization and adrenaline, "were going to beat it" and so on. And you just get caught up in the fight. And then the treatment ends. When the treatment stops there is uncertainty. "What is going to happen"? "Is it elsewhere in my body"? "Will it come back"? And that is a very real thing with cancer because that, in fact, is often what does happen.

Once the patient and family get a clean bill of health after the treatment ends, the family tries to get their lives back together. They try to put the cancer behind them even though everyone has doubts and fears. And that's fine until a recurrence comes. And that's when there is

11

another crisis point. Now, the patient has been worrying all along if the cancer is going to come back. Every check-up is filled with anxiety—the six-week, three-month, six-month anxiety and uncertainty that they live with. Every cold they get, they wonder if it is in my lungs. Every headache, is it a brain tumor? This is what the patient's and families live with. Nobody is saying this, but that's the backdrop, really.

You are never the same. Every little twinge could be a reminder. But having said that, as the months and years elapse, there is more of a sense that the crisis is behind you. But if recurrence occurs then you are really in for some serious stuff. The family regroups and tries to maintain some optimism. But depending upon how the treatment goes, how sick the patient becomes, that's when you are really going to get some depression and the impact of it is going to sink in.

For example, we have a family now in our bereavement group where the mother died of lung cancer. She was fifty-three. She had a wonderful prognosis from the beginning. And so the family's hopes were based on the initial information. Then the cancer recurred and the doctors were still saying good things. It came back a third time and they were still saying hopeful things—"We got it this time." But then she died and the family was totally surprised and devastated.

When the person does die, family members can enter into a bereavement group. Bereavement is the end of the line. Relief is one feeling, particularly the ones that have been through a long drawn out thing with cancer. There is a feeling of relief that the person is no longer in pain that the suffering is over. Prior to death, pain is really a big issue. The fear is that the pain may be overwhelming. Not that the patients won't have pain, but that it will be overwhelming and relentless, that to them is more terrifying than death.

Bereavement is filled with many different things. There's initially a feeling of tremendous shock and disbelief, even as you watch a person die over many months. You can understand the shock and disbelief in an accident, but when you watch a person die from cancer, the shock and disbelief is still enormous. We just can't comprehend death, you know? We just can't get a handle on it. We just can't get that they're not here, and where are they? And what happened? And you go through the burial, and you just can't get a handle on it, you know? And that shock and numbness persists for a long time, but then other things come in. Grief has its own path that takes over the course of a year or longer. I think the shock and numbness is nature's way of protecting families, initially. And then little by little that wears off, and the reality begins to set in, then the full-fledged grief begins. The anger, and the sadness, and the loneliness, and the lack of energy, and the tiredness, the pain in the chest, and the stomach distress, and the headaches and all the physical, somatic things that attend bereavement, and are part of the grief process. Your whole world is turned upside down. You don't know which end is which, and you just kind of wander in a maze or a dream. Life, life always is pushing you along and intruding, and you have to deal with things, but basically you're out of it for the longest time. And you go through all kinds of ups and downs. It's not a static thing. It goes on much longer than people imagine. The whole first year is a washout. The end result of the grief process is to find meaning in life, and that takes a long time because of the shattering, the unfairness, the injustice, the feeling of being left behind, all of that. But I think people who come to the group may self-reflect. The ones that come to the group I find are successful in the resolution of their grief.

They find meaning in their life after death. I don't know how other people handle grief without a support group. You can tough it out, I guess, but there will not be the same kind of healing as when you deal with it. The group gives the person permission to grieve. It really is a support. It gives them time to grieve. It's okay to feel lousy, it's okay to feel angry, it's okay to stay in bed all day, it's okay to be furious with God, and it's okay to go the grave and cry. People will spend typically anywhere from six months to about a year in a group. It's interesting to see people who have stayed in the group for a long time move through the stages. I don't want to suggest that grief is like a stage, but you can see them move from the numbness and the disbelief, into the heart of the grief. And that goes on for a long, long time. You see them struggle with lots of things.

So the group gives people permission to experience all the dimensions of their grief, which is, again, not available to them outside. You know, friends and neighbors say to a group member after two months away from the group, "Let's go to Atlantic City," or "Let's go see the Knicks." They have no idea. Two months and you're just starting to get into the grief. The Knicks? What are you . . . Who gives a shit about basketball? (laughs) I like it when people are ready to leave the group. You can see that there's a little spark, a little energy, a little more interest in life.

I'm starting my third year as an oncology social worker. I've been at the _____ for over two years now. Prior to that, I've been a social worker since 1981, ten years. And I've had a variety of different experiences. I've worked in a family service agency, I've worked in the alcoholism field, women's health center, and I had a private practice. You want the truth? I was trying to straighten out my own life. I was having certain personal problems. I got some very good help along the way and in the process I found out that I had a real interest in it, and the potential to do the work myself. It has been a growing commitment and process. Yes I do find that most people get into a profession like social work or helping people because of something that happened to them. They may not admit it, but I sometimes see people drawn into the profession to try and solve problems of their own—some kind of loss, or a personal situation that draws them to the work.

I don't know exactly where the idea to work in oncology came from. Well, I know partly where it came from. The Simonton's book, *Getting Well Again,* interested me when I graduated from school. And I was very involved with different kinds of social work, and I thought, "Oh, boy, I'd love to do that, work with cancer patients, wouldn't that be great."

I spent a long time looking for work in the cancer field. And I wasn't hired. I couldn't find anything. I was looking in various institutions, and all the doors were closed at the time. It was 10 years later that the opportunity to work in oncology actually came to me. During this time I was involved with other kinds of social work, the birth of my son, and taking care of him. Really (laughs) I had a lot of growing before I could come into this work. My view back then was so naïve. I thought I was gonna help people get better. And my work has not turned out to be like that at all. It really hasn't turned out to be that at all. So, when I was finishing up the time I had taken off to raise my son, I saw an ad in the paper for this place, and I applied, and I got the job, and here I am.

Our organization is set up primarily to take care of the needs of patients and families. We were thinking in a very practical way initially. When people are diagnosed with cancer they have to handle so many different things. Almost immediately they're deluged with questions about insurance coverage, medical forms, money needed, where to get a wig, if they need nursing care, or childcare, a host of questions come up. And, of course, as the illness progresses, needs often change. So we function as a kind of a clearing-house for people to come to find out what's available, because most people don't know where to get help especially with kinds of grants and entitlements and insurance, problems with home care and nursing care. So, in a very practical way we help people with those kinds of things all the time. And then we also recognize the emotional, and psychological and spiritual impact that cancer has on patients and families. So, we have many programs for patients and families. I would say that our support groups probably are the backbone of the program, where people come and talk and share their experience, and try and make sense of it. And I'm active in leading groups. In general, no, I don't find that most people are fearful of talking about death and dying, and loss. Members who are already part of a group talk about it. New people coming in are sometimes hesitant to partake, but I've found people to be very open to talk about death and dying. And they're relieved. They're relieved to talk about it because they have no opportunity to do it in their private lives, for the most part. Why? Well, within the family one of the things that I've observed is that, if a member of the family gets cancer it's a subject that's really avoided. The husband doesn't want to talk to the wife for fear of upsetting her. Say the wife is the patient. The wife doesn't want to talk to the husband for fear of upsetting him. None of them wants to talk to the kids, for fear of upsetting them. So, a kind of dance begins, in which people privately think about the disease but publicly it's hard for them to say anything.

It's more likely the patient will raise the issue of death, rather than the family member; when the patient raises the issue of death the family member says, "Oh, no, what do you mean? You're gonna make it. What are you talking about?" And that just stops the conversation, you see. That stops the conversation. It seems to me that the family member experiences denial in order to survive, because they have to deal with the horror and devastation of that day-by-day care, watching someone they love die. I was just on the phone with a woman today who had gone through this with her husband. He was not even 50, this guy, and they'd been married 23 years and have two kids, and he died about two weeks ago. I met them right in the beginning. The horror of watching someone you love, a big strapping person in this case, get sick, and sicker, become more debilitated, and watch that whole process right to the death. It's just unbelievable. So in order for them to go on, the caregiver, the person taking care of the family and the person that's sick, really needs to be in a state of denial. I don't know if there's a term "positive denial," but that's my own little word that I'm using to describe this situation—it's denial in the service of enabling them to do what they have to do. In other words, it's not denial in the sense that they're out of touch with reality. It's a healthy kind of denial, which enables them to go on. So when the patient says, "I don't think I'm gonna make it," or "I wonder where all this is going?" the caretaker, more or less, stops these thoughts. They can't deal with whatever feelings that would come up if the person says, "I'm going to die," or "I think I'm going to die." I think that's unfortunate, when the conversation is short-circuited.

Sometimes people need help in order to have that conversation. I've been able to open up the topic for people when they come here because I'll ask them. If I'm seeing a couple, or I'm seeing a patient, or I'm seeing a family member, or maybe the mother and the children and the husband separately, I'll ask them. I'll ask them right out, just like that. What are they thinking about? What are they saying? Are they talking to each other? I particularly encourage couples to have an ending, to have a good-bye. I encourage them to say all the things they want to say. So, I can help in that sense, I can open it up and make it okay for them to go do what they have to do.

How do I do that? Just by creating a safe environment. In this instance, the woman whose husband had multiple myeloma, which is a terrible diagnosis from the get-go, had problems: deteriorated very rapidly. He could not and did not want to deal with the question of death. It was very hard for him. I saw him privately and let it float out there, and he was a very strong and proud man. And I really respect the idea that people be allowed to handle this experience in whatever way they can. However they get to it is fine with me. This has been sort of a humbling experience for me in terms of limitations about who I am and what my work is all about. I don't have any answers to this question. I don't have any ideas how people get through this experience. However they get through it—if they can talk about it fine, if they can't talk about it, that's also fine. If they're in denial, so be it. If they're open to it, so be it. So, I see my role very differently in terms of how I'm interacting with patients.

I come to this work forever as a student. I have not experienced this kind of trauma in my life. I have not experienced this at all. I have healthy parents and grandparents who have lived long lives without any devastating illnesses. I have no idea what the impact would be, how I would react. I have no answers. What I realize now about the meaning of the work, has been clarified in the process of super-vising some graduate students in social work. These students are very concerned and preoccupied with how they are doing, what kind of work they are doing, and how to measure it. Are they helping people? Is change taking place? And feeling that nothing is happening. What I think now is that showing up is 90 percent of the work; the courage that it takes to come and sit with people who are dying and let them talk is the gift. You see, allowing them to talk is the gift and the work because they don't have the opportunity to talk about it in their private lives.

I think this culture is in a state of denial about death and dying. I think we are so enamored of medical technology and what medicine can do, and the promise that it holds for us, that it is very hard to acknowledge that death is a part of life, and that it is not a medical failure necessarily. I think this is very ingrained in our society.

How do I deal with my own mortality? Oh, my goodness. Well it's not easy. I'll tell you on some levels it's extremely frightening because I can no longer, at least intellectually, entertain the thought that bad things will not happen in my family. It could be me as well as the next guy. And I know that is true deep inside, so, it forces me into a kind of philosophical, spiritual awareness. I attended a conference once on grief and loss, and a really marvelous fellow talked about existential angst, when you realize there's no place to put your feet on the ground and that you're suspended somewhere in midair. You recognize the randomness of the universe, and the unfairness of the universe and the unpredictability. So, most of the time you have to block that out, and I think it's wonderful to be able to block that out. Do you know what I mean? Yes, that's the healthy denial. But in my work I confront it every day. I can't block it out. But, I do take care of myself, emotionally, spiritually, and physically. I find opportunities to handle the grief part of my work. I make sure that there's support in my life outside of work and good experiences. I have supervision for my own work. I'm involved in yoga and I work out, I like to garden, cook, and go to movies. Yeah, absolutely, I think one has to have balance.

I also find workshops and conferences to be very, very helpful because it's replenishment. There's sharing of information with colleagues and a sense of not working in isolation because you draw on the support of other people and their experiences. I think if you don't have all that the potential for burnout is really pretty great. I haven't experienced much of that, so far.

Mark: What would happen if you ever came down with cancer?

Cindy: This is a personal book. (Laughs) Umm . . . I think I would first want to acknowledge that this could be the end of my life. Cancer is not necessarily a death sentence. But if I got cancer, I would want to acknowledge that this cancer could be the beginning of the end of my life. That's where I would start, as opposed to "I'm gonna beat this thing, I'm gonna beat this thing, I'm gonna beat this thing." But I'm also a fighter so I would investigate and find out as much information as I could. I'm a very informed medical consumer, and I would make decisions with the help of my family, but there would be the knowledge that underneath, I don't know where it's going. I can only conceive of it in terms of a spiritual journey because cancer patients I know live with uncertainty. I mean, to me there is nothing worse than living with the uncertainty. I share this based on conversations with many people in support groups who talk about the uncertainty of not knowing what will happen, and when; how much time you have; are you going to deteriorate? Are you going to get better? Will there be pain? You live with that uncertainty all the time.

Mark: I think that uncertainty you're talking about is prevalent with every single person in everyday life.

Cindy: Yeah, but we're able to block it out, though.

Mark: That's the denial process.

Cindy: That's exactly right. But to live with that full knowledge, you'd go crazy, though. You know, your kid could be kidnapped, or that . . .

Mark: You can't go around with that. You'd be crippled.

Cindy: You'd be crippled.

Mark: But all I'm trying to say is that it's there.

Cindy: Yes.

Mark: That it's always there.

Cindy: Right.

Mark: No matter what you do.

Cindy: Right.

Mark: And that's why we need the healthy illusions, we need the healthy denial, so we can live.

Cindy: Right.

Mark: Because the paradox of life and death is so overwhelming that you've got to be able to balance it, and that's what, the quote, existential philosophy is all about.

Yeah, and that's why I have so much respect for my patients, because they have to live with that. They don't have the illusions anymore. They have to live with the paradox and the unknown and the uncertainty. Shattering is the best way to describe it. My work begins when the shattering has occurred. The way I view the work now, the work that we do here at the _____, is to help people acknowledge that shattering, and to begin to pick up the pieces of their life in a very ordinary and mundane way, to continue to live, to continue to cope.

I don't use any methods to get them to continue to live. In a sense, and I know other people might take a different view, I don't see my job as getting them to do anything. I don't see it as my job to get them to take their medication, or to get them to not be depressed, or to get them to talk to people, or get them to do any other thing. I guess the way I conceive of my job is as a journey, and I'm with them on their path. That's the best way I can conceive of it. And I'm with them as they receive whatever information they receive. And that's, that's enough, if you know what I mean. They can decide for themselves. I mean, we talk about a lot of things and explore things, and I'll illuminate things and I ask them things, but basically I acknowledge things for them. I don't try to cheer them up; I don't try to make them feel less depressed. I just try to acknowledge the full state of depression, and I think it's comforting in a way because people don't get this experience outside.

Not only is there kind of denial of death on the outside, but people also want you to feel well. They want you to feel good and be happy. And sometimes they're not. And I think cancer patients need to feel that it's okay to be bummed out, and pissed off by it to be discouraged by it and to be all of the things you see. And then what happens is people will move on their own. In other words, if the feeling is fully experienced, it will evolve into something else. You know life is so strange, it goes from elation to boredom to frustration to annoyance just in the course of your day or in the course of being a cancer patient. And people's lives are very much in process, they're in relationships, and whatever crap they've been dealing with, that's all there, and then there's cancer on top of it. And often times the life stuff is what they're really dealing with, you know, the unresolved stuff in their marriage, the estrangement from a child, being underpaid at work, whatever the concerns, that keep going on. And often that's the thing that really fuels them every day.

No, I don't work closely with physicians during this process. I hate to generalize, but not many doctors make referrals to us, and I'm affiliated with two hospitals. Even our own medical directors don't make referrals to us. Occasionally they send a referral, but they see hundreds and hundreds of patients. People find out about us from the newspaper, word of mouth, they call up Cancer Care; they go sometimes to the end of the earth to find us. These are not ogres, these doctors. These are not men who are emotionally insensitive, who are not caring, who don't understand the impact of the experience. These are real human beings. It's a mystery. You know I understand the way in which medicine is practiced today. They don't have time to do this kind of work, to have empathy and be emotionally available to the patient and the families. They don't have time to do it because you can't sit down with a patient, get them started, and then in ten minutes say, "Sorry, I have to see the next person." We have the time to do this. I have the luxury of time. And you do need time. You need an hour. You need an hour just to get started. So, I thought it would make a nice marriage, if they could say to their patients and families, "Look, I'm going to take care of this part, but I want you to go over to the _____. I want you to visit them. I want you to go find out what they are about and get involved with their groups. If you need anybody to talk too individually, Cindy is over there." They could just point them in the direction. Maybe it's a function of specialization and training that they see cancer as tumor in a body and that's it. They're not seeing the emotional, social, and psychological eruption of cancer, the impact of it in their patient's lives. The patient will say, "Well, you know, to you, doctor, cancer is an everyday event, but to me it's all new."

I think the patients are very angry because of the lack of a human connection with the doctor. It's the lack of acknowledgment of a patient being a unique individual. The doctor fails to acknowledge their personhood, their humanity. Patients want to have the most technologically trained doctor. They want that. And that's well and good. I think they could live with the doctor the way he is—pressured for time, and not having a good beside manner, and so forth. I think they could deal with that if the doctor in some way acknowledges what they're going through.

Some doctors are now moving toward this. A practice where they're actually hiring a social worker or a nurse to be part of the practice, so that patients can be seen on-site to deal with some of the psycho-social issues. I met a woman at an oncology convention, who is a social worker, who was hired full-time by a radiologist to be in her office to deal with patients and families. I mean that's a wonderful model.

I'll tell you something. I have a friend who is in medical school now. She is 36 years old and studying at Brown. She has three children and worked in the medical setting as an occupational therapist for many years. Her father is a doctor.

She has a lot of experience in life and the world. She talks to me often about the process in which medical students are brainwashed and desensitized. While it's true there are more women in medical school, Umm, if they are getting those kids straight out of college without any life experience, in some ways they will be desensitized and brainwashed in the same ways as the male doctor. Hopefully the nurturing qualities women bring will help overcome that, but practicing in an institutional setting is very hard. It's very hard for the nurses to overcome the setting with whatever caring, empathic responses they have. They operate within an institution that makes it so hard to extend the kind of care that you would like to. And my friend is forever fighting. I mean, she will speak up and challenge these old farts that have been in medical school for a hundred years. She will bring in real life examples, "What about this? And doctor, why are you not working with the team in the hospital? Why have you not brought in pastoral care? Why have you not brought in a social worker? Why did you do this and not do this?"

Yeah, it does anger me. I experience frustrations. I have enough work to do here and I'm clear about what my work is and I choose to work in a personal, particular way. I do not get involved in policy kind of things. I know people who are cut out for that, and I applaud them. But my work is on a very personal level.

I think I will be doing this for a long time. One thing that I feel fortunate with the work is that my patient contact is balanced with some other things professionally, which I really enjoy. I supervise students, I get to write, I get to do some public relations work, and I get to do some training work. I've also been working with nurses in the different hospitals doing workshops on grief and loss, cancer and sexuality and, so, as long as those other, different parts of me are used professionally, that I like. So it's a balance to the work. But the heart and soul of it for me is the patient care. I would not be doing those other things if I did not like the work with the patients.

I've been lucky finding balance in my own life so I can continue to do the work. I will not burn myself out. Throughout my social work career I have established a balance between what I feel I can do, you know the psychic energy that I can use to do the work, and what I need for myself, and my family.

You know it's very hard to convey the richness of this work and the feelings of satisfaction and the profound feeling I have of privilege to do the work. I'm not overstating the case. I've done many things in social work before, and this is really the most moving of all. I think because it's a special opportunity to connect with people. The prospect of death I think really cuts through rather quickly many of the details, and little bits and pieces and ways in which we weave our lives together to protect ourselves. You get a sense of what I'm talking about? It just cuts through all illusions. I guess the word I would use to describe it is a potential for intimacy. For real intimacy. So, I find that relationships develop quickly. Trust is established quickly, more quickly than in other situations. There's more of an openness or a willingness to really examine one's life. Whatever spiritual or religious inclinations or yearnings are there, they come to the fore because psychologically and spiritually, and emotionally, cancer shatters things and cracks open your ideas about the nature of the world and your place in it. It shatters your sense of invulnerability. You, all of us, myself included, really think that bad things are not going to happen to us, and to the people that we love, that it's going to be someone else. And that if death comes, I'll be one hundred and four, and I'll die in my sleep. But cancer changes all of that. After the diagnosis of cancer, life is changed irrevocably. Irrevocably. It is not as before. And it is profound, because it brings to the front of your awareness for the first time you own mortality. That's it. It brings that to mind.

One of the things quelling this existential angst is a sense that things are preordained. In my bereavement group I hear stories like, "You know, my husband had fifty-three years of life and that was it. No more, no less. He had his time, and he lived out his time." And something like that is beginning to form in my mind.

In a sense I do not know how much time I have, I don't know how much time my family has. I have time, and all I can do is live that out. Yeah, all I can do is live that out. I've been dealt this hand, and I don't know what cards are coming my way. It seems like a good hand so far. I've watched other people get dealt rotten hands and deal with it, and come through. Yeah, I think it's kind of inspiring. You can't control what hand you're dealt, or when it's dealt, but you pick up the pieces when you get that hand. You pick up the damn hand and you play it out. You know, I think that's a good analogy for this cancer work. You get dealt the hand and you play it out however you can.

*   *   *

I'm was often struck by Cindy's extraordinary detail in describing what it means to live with cancer and unwavering dedication and compassion toward her patients and their families.

After tracking Cindy down last year to thank her for helping get this book published, she told me there was a sense of unreality that accompanied her entire experience as an oncology social worker. You go through everything but it feels unreal, she said.

Cindy stopped being an oncology social worker a few years after our interview in order to take care of her newborn son Matthew. After four years of raising her second child, Cindy was unable to find another oncology position. She now works as a social worker within Head Start, the government educational program. In April of 1999, Cindy's world turned "unreal" once again, as her husband was diagnosed with leukemia. He is now thankfully in remission.

JEFF

You know, as a culture, we expect everybody to jog, lift weights, and to wear Reeboks, and to look like what's her name, Christy Brinkley, or Cindy Crawford, that kind of thing. So, to be sick is almost taboo. I mean a lot of people don't even like calling in sick, they'd rather go to work sick. Which is like a, right, a weakness, which is a miniature version of this fear of death. And the patients will say that very clearly. They'll say, "I was a mother, I was working, I was successful at this, I never needed anything from anybody." I mean people go through this, whatever their disability or even just old age, but with cancer I think it's all the more so because cancer takes away your feeling of control, you know, being the master of your own destiny, so to speak. One young man in a support group spoke about the cancer train. He said, "You get the diagnosis, you get on the train and it's a runaway train. You don't know where the train is going to go, but you cannot get off the train." Other people haven't put it the same way, but basically, once you have a diagnosis of cancer your peace of mind is taken. It's like being a rape victim or a mugging victim, something like that. There's a sense of violation. One woman said it felt to her like the two things felt very similar, because some stranger came into her life and messed up her sense of security.

I've been an oncology social worker since November 1990. Yes, relatively new. Well, I was a special education teacher, and taught mainly head start programs for about six years. It was kind of a two-pronged thing. Number one, I had always thought about being a psychotherapist, and the best route for that, for me, was to get the MSW. I wanted to work with families and children. I would see that I would work with them up to a certain level. I'd get the kids to a certain level and then I would kind of hit a wall with the family. And then I realized they would hit their wall with the outside society, government agencies, whatever. So, that made me want to get into social work. I kind of ended up at the hospital just by a fluke, because a school I was suppose to work at didn't open. It was a brand new school and never came to be. I interviewed here for a psychiatric social worker job to cover somebody on maternity leave, and they ended up giving that position to somebody else, but apparently they liked me. They called me a few months later and said would I like to be the oncology social worker. I hemmed and hawed, and thought about it and eventually decided yes.

I decided to do it because of partly who I am as a person. I was brought up a Quaker, and so I've always had a very strong spiritual part of my life, or at least wanted to. And, Umm, you know, there has been a lot of thought, of course, about the spiritual side of life. Feeling, and that kind of thing. I myself haven't had a personal experience with cancer, but my mother's mother died of cancer when she was young, and my father's father died of cancer just a little while before I was born. So, like every family, pretty much every family, I have some history of it in my family. And, I just thought of them, and said, well, I'm interested in the spiritual side of life and I guess this in kind of like a door that is open to me. This would be, it's kind of like, you know, they say if you can live in New York you can live anywhere. So I said to myself, if I could do oncology social work that will really prepare me for really doing some very intense, umm, personal and spiritual based work as a therapist.

Can I describe the general philosophy I bring into oncology? Sure. Well, basically, in a nutshell, it's that death is a continuing of life. I don't know if I believe in reincarnation, or not. I don't know if I believe in heaven as such. But I certainly believe in an afterlife, and I believe that death is a door to the next stage, and that it is not a bad thing, you know. I don't know how I'll feel when it comes time for my own death. I might change my mind. Or that of my parents, or whatever, but that's my philosophy. So, I guess I see my role in working with the terminally ill as helping that process, helping the patient and the family accept the dying process, and making it as comfortable on all different levels as I can.

Well, yeah, I guess I've been successful in that. If someone comes to me wanting me to make him or her comfortable, I have to really find out where they are, so to speak. That is what the social worker does to start with a client. So, if I'm talking with a patient, I have to start even with what their knowledge base is. Do they know they have cancer? Do they know, if the answer to that is yes, how serious it is? And each case is going to be different. You know patients will say I don't have cancer, I just have a tumor. Or I have a tumor that is benign. They will say these different things that apparently their family will have told them. There is a lot of misinformation that the patients get. And I can't really tell them no, that is not true you actually have terminal liver cancer. I can't, that's not within my parameters to give them the information, so I have to start with what they know. And, I will try to lead with the truth, like, have you spoken to your doctor, or how have you been feeling. Whatever they tell me they have I'll take at face value, and I'll explore it with them. Because they might say to me oh, you know I just have a little tumor, or something like that, which makes it sound like they feel the situation is better. But, then the next thing will be I'm scared, or I'm afraid, or that I think I haven't been told everything. Or, I can't understand the doctor, he won't tell me, or people are acting strange to me, you know, whatever. There will be some clue from the patient that they are uneasy. So, I'll say, well, what would you like to do about the information. Would you like to talk with the doctor? You're the patient; it's your right. I'll try to steer them toward as much information as possible, because I feel that they should know.

Well, see, legally the doctor should tell. It is the patient's right to know, patients bill of rights is very clear about that. But, if a doctor or nurse—the doctor usually sets the pace—the doctor usually doesn't have that good of comfort level with talking to people about terminal illness, or even prognosis or diagnosis of cancer, then you kind of have to go to the family. But, usually it is the family themselves who—the most frequent thing that I've heard is that if Uncle Joe knows he has terminal cancer it will kill him, which obviously is not logical. And they say it, and believe it when they say it. That knowledge itself, that hearing of words, will kill the patient.

Oh yes, it's denial. I would say it is in a least a third, maybe half of my experiences. I'll give you a typical scenario. The patient is an 83-year-old woman who lives alone, and has two adult daughters. They live outside the city and they want her to go to a nursing home, which is in of itself a whole other area we could get into some other time. But, she doesn't know her diagnosis. So, I'm sitting with the adult daughters and talking to them. She doesn't know, and she can't know about her illness. I'll say:

(Jeff): Well, what does she know, what is her understanding?

(Daughter(s)): Well, she just thinks she needs to get some tests. She thinks that she has an ulcer.

Jeff: Okay, what does she say about her health? Does she ever say anything about being afraid?

Daughters: Well, yeah, now that you mention it, she will say things like, well as long as it isn't cancer.

Jeff: Well, obviously it's on her mind. How do you thing she got it on her mind?

Daughters: Oh, I don't know, maybe she's just worried.

Jeff: What else does she say?

Daughters: Oh, she'll say things, the funniest things, she'll say things like, don't leave me, don't let me die, don't leave me to die alone, don't put me in a nursing home to die alone. Oh, Mom, you what are you talking about. Your not gonna die, your fine.

Jeff: You're telling me that she's talking about cancer. She's talking about dying. Don't you think that she knows? It is her own body. She must be able to feel it herself, that she is very sick.

Sometimes they'll say "no," or whatever. But then they'll say, "Yeah, I guess." And I say, "Ok, so what your telling me is that you know, she knows, and you that she knows and she knows that you know. But, yet, you're not talking about it." Why is this? Well it goes back to this; this kind of myth that I guess we have that words themselves will kill. It's like the opposite of sticks and stones will hurt my bones, but names will never hurt me. When I get them to that impasse I'll say, "But, isn't this a terrible thing because here your are, really thinking my mom has only a little time left, and yet you can't really talk about anything of importance because your hiding this thing from each other. Don't you feel like that's an isolating thing?" And sometimes, and sometimes I'm able to get the families to say, "You know, your right. She should know, and it's going to be hard." And then they'll usually get the doctor to go in and tell the family. And then I'll do damage control with the family, the patient, and kids. Oh yes, there is a communication problem here. How do we break these communication barriers?

Well, I guess what I've been saying is, what I try to do is help all the parties involved see kind of the bigger picture. In other words, say, because the doctor has a feeling that if he or she loses a patient, that he or she has failed, Umm . . . I remember an oncologist, who was one of the oncology fellows, moved on to his own practice saying to me "I don't kill patients." Meaning that somehow all his patients just lived. And not too long after hearing that statement, we had a situation which a very young patient of his, a woman I believe about 37 years of age, had very serious gastric cancer. A very, very sick woman; we wanted her to go home with a hospice program, but he had her on a type of feeding that is very aggressive. They call the treatment TPM. And he could not understand that, number one, the TPM was feeding the cancer, rather than feeding the patient. And I'm not a medical person, but I came to understand this. He could understand it, but he couldn't assimilate it, and he couldn't quite understand the idea of hospice because he felt that she had a very good chance. But he as the quote, professional person unquote was not able to separate his own fear of death, and I think fear of failure.

The cases of younger people have also affected me personally. In that I would find myself, you know, hoping against hope that this young woman with three kids would somehow be it, or at least live long enough to put something together for her kids. And that gets into the whole another story, the whole systemic thing, yes the business side, the insurance side. We can come back to that. Yeah, I have been affected, and it's not only with the younger people, but it seems like with certain patients and families. Maybe the ones that were more open to me, so I reciprocated, I don't know. I can't, I don't know what the X factor is, but there's certain families that, patients that I have felt closer to. I haven't gone to any funerals. I know of people who have done that. To me, I don't know, my sense of boundaries is that I'm not going to do that. I certainly have some cause, and have received mass cards, and it's kind of, well, not funny, of course, but when I first started here and a patient would die, I would write a closing note that would go on the medical chart. I would say, "Patient died, whatever, awaiting nursing home placement." I would say, "Case closed. God rest his soul." Or "God rest her soul." And to me that was like a little sense of closure. At that point it didn't matter if I was close to them or not, it just seemed like the Christian thing to do. Uh, I was told that it was unprofessional, and that I could not show the documentation. We are professionals and we do not integrate our religious or personal vies into the medical record, which is a legal document. So, needless to say I didn't feel too happy about that. But, again, that goes into this universal denial thing. I guess, you know, we are part of a medical model; you see the patient as patient diseased, and that's it, we don't talk about it as if it were a human and someone with a soul.

How well do I cope with all this? Well, I have to say that it has really depended on a lot of different things. For a long time it was very hard for me to breathe properly with patients because I bought into this whole professional type thing. Yeah, I cut myself off, but I always did something. For awhile I had a miniature Zen rock garden and people would say what's that for, and I would say well it's like a memorial for all the patients that have died. I would find that I do a lot of it as I'm going. For example, I would speak to a patient or to a family member and I'm running down the stairwell to go to the next place just doing a little sign of the cross, and saying "God have mercy on my soul." That helps, you know as long as I'm praying that's the main thing. I feel like that's helping me to feel again. That I'm making the best of it, and that my concerns and care for people are coming out. Sometimes I just can't help it and I will cry. I do that in as private a way as I can, you know. But I think with the group, being that is a more informal type thing, and although quasi-connected with the hospital, its not done there with everyone around. The group I'm referring to is the cancer patient family group that I co-lead. I'm able to be freer with my feelings there and talk about them more. Every once in awhile I will pray to God and I'll say, "You know, God, if you really expect me to be able to do this then you are going to have send me more strength. You're going to have to, you know, help me to deal with this." Because I'm only 32 years old and I'm surrounded by all these dying people. This is very heavy for me, you know. Give me a break. But you know doing that makes me feel better, as well. As long as I know I'm not coping with this myself. Yeah, there is something moral, cosmic, something much larger that keeps it together for me. My fiancée, whom I met here at the hospital, she was an oncology volunteer, that's how we met, is someone I can also talk about it. She and I would talk sometimes about members of the group that have passed. Somewhat to my colleagues and my co-leaders are also very emotionally open about the things.

Yeah, support systems are important and it does help. Well, yes and no whether or not physicians and nurses have this support system. From what I can see the physicians have a stiff-upper lip way of supporting each other. One way that they do it is they speak about the patients as symptoms, attaching all these different terms. Sometimes I sit in these tumor rounds; it's amazing. They'll say about three words that indicate it's a human being. I guess if I dealt with it every single day, with that sort of responsibility, you know, maybe that's what I would do. Yeah, just to survive. I don't think that the physicians have a support group. Some of them are deeply religious, I think, but I'm not sure. Nurses had a support group that I co-led, but that disbanded after a while because people didn't have time to do it. Well, I guess it was the same kind of taboo, that, you know, we are professional people, and we don't talk about the emotional side of it. I mean it's true, it is uncomfortable to really talk about or express your sorrow in a professional place.

Well, the nurses, I think, they are able to see their role as a comforting role, and as providing the best care possible. I think they have less trouble, which is why, I think, they were able to fit into a support group as it was happening. And I think if there were one now, I'm sure that they would attend. The physicians, like I said before they kind of put themselves in a no-win situation because if your main goal is to stop people from dying then you can't be successful, because people will die. I mean they might not die this year, but they will die. And I see some doctors that are able to work with that and are able to say, "Ok, lets' help them be more comfortable." The thing is, again from doing the support groups, some cancer patients, survivors, come to the support groups having had no treatment at all, and have not needed any. I mean there's people who need treatment and don't get it. I'll get into that, but people who have maybe a type of lymphoma that hasn't been surgically removed, hasn't received any chemotherapy or anything, and they come to the support group for years because they say, "What if, what if it blows up." People who are cancer-free, who had it all eradicated, and who have may be minute traces left, what if?

Mark: It's always in the back of their minds.

That's the cancer train. You don't get off once you're on. Doesn't matter if the cancer is gone. We, who have not had cancer, really cannot, really can't imagine. I mean even I, who listen to all these stories, talking to people, and having empathized, still it's unimaginable. It's unimaginable because it really does take away that sense that we all have of immortality. And even though I might say to you philosophically, "Oh, you know, death is a door that opens, and blah, blah, blah." You tell me, I don't know if I could still be quite so philosophical, you know. You know, I think that sort of philosophy is kind of a luxury that we have. And in a way, that philosophy in of itself is a buffer against the fear of death.

My point of view has become that everyone will do what works for them. I've had people who have come to the hospital with a very early diagnosis. Very treatable situation and they've not taken treatment. And then I've seen them again, a year and half later, and they really should have taken some treatment because the cancer has, of course, spread. That is usually with younger folks. And that's what people call denial.

Those people are still holding onto in their heads their immortality. But in a way that is literally killing them. I'll tell a brief story.

There was this woman who wanted me to see about a radiation clinic, because she didn't want to accept any sort of treatment. She believed a miracle from God would cure her. So here we were sitting in this very serious situation and I said, "You're going to think I'm crazy, but I'm going to tell you a joke." And I said, "Umm, there was this very religious man who spoke to God all the time and felt truly that God had singled him out and was very close to him. A flood was coming and this man was in his house; people came up with a car and they said, "Your house is going to be flooded, let us drive you to higher ground." The man responded "Oh no, no, no God will take care of me, I don't need that." So, when the waters came up, and they were up to his porch they came in a boat and they said, "Come on, let us take you to higher ground." "Oh no, the man responded, God has been speaking to me and he said he was going to take care of me." And so finally the water was up to his roof and the guy is on top of the roof. And then the helicopter comes and they say, "Come on, this is your last chance. Let us take you away." And he said the same thing; "No, no, God will take care of me." Then the water comes and the guy drowns, and he goes to heaven and he says to God, "God, you know, what's the story? I thought I was your special person. How come you didn't save me?" And God said, "What do you want from me? I send a car, I sent a boat, I sent a helicopter and you turned it all away."

I told her this joke at this very serious moment to show her that, look, for all you know, the radiation could be the miracle. She heard what I was saying, but she still wouldn't come to treatment. I don't know, what can you do? I don't know what to do. I don't know. That's the whole thing. Part of my job sometimes has been to convince people not to take treatment because I feel that, that's their prerogative. I'm just trying to help them almost to choose the chance to live over certain death.

Just last week I had a very interesting conversation. The official response to it was good because she spoke for about 45 minutes and was saying that the cancer is in her life and that she knows it's pretty much the end, ok? Basically, she spoke mostly about the fact that she had to put on a brave front for her two children, who were adults about my age. The kids would be saying things like, "Mom, you can't die, we can't live without you, blah, blah . . . I'd say it sounds like denial, whatever. This is what they were saying. She was basically saying the fight was gone. She said she had, had cancer for nine years. And I thought nine years? She said she ". . . was doing great, but now it's come back, and I don't have the fight anymore, but I feel like I'm supposed to." We talked for a while, and then she said to me, "Well, I guess it's natural, everybody thinks about it sometime." And I said, "Thinks about what?" And she said,

"You know, ending it all." And I said, "Well, I guess you have been thinking about it." And then she proceeded to talk to me about suicide and how society would say it's cowardly, but really it's a courageous thing to end your own life. And I said, "What would you do?" "Well, I couldn't take pills because I wouldn't know which ones to take, and I'd probably make myself sick, but if really wanted to, I know how I could get my hands on a gun." Eventually, we finished the conversation and I put a note on the chart saying, "Psychiatrist, please see this woman because she is having suicidal ideation, and that it's understandable given the diagnosis." The doctor told me that he spent 45 minutes with her and she never said anything about suicide. I said, "Well, maybe our training is different. She says different things to different people." He said that she mentioned to him that sometimes people will talk fantasy; it means a cry of help, to get people to care for them, something like that. But in his note he didn't mention it either. I was looking at this within the world of denial and taboo. The ultimate taboo, I guess, is to think about suicide. No, she left the hospital and as far as I know is still alive.

Over the course of either my training or of things I have experienced, I certainly had people tell me yes, that they'd been thinking about it. Mainly patients, though. I can't think off hand of many professionals. But human nature being what it is, I'm sure. But this was the first time in this setting, doing oncology that it was this clear. And it wasn't just because someone saying, "Oh, I don't know if it's worth it." This woman at that moment, seemed to me like she could. You do hear a lot about this in the group. You hear people thinking about it, but mainly talking themselves out of it. Within the group there is a wide range tolerance about what you do. In the groups there are a lot of people who want to soothe. The want to say, oh you'll be okay, it will be better. You have to keep positive thinking. And cancer patients, as a whole, are sick to death of being told to think positively by people who don't have cancer. They would like to be told that I have no idea what you are going through, but whatever you want to tell me, tell me, and we'll face it together. And whatever I can to for you, I'll do. A lot of times its just little kindness.

Yes, exactly, it could be just about anybody. They say don't tell me how to feel. Listen to how I feel. And I have a life; I'm not just a cancer patient. I am a person with cancer. I had a situation in which a woman had a new diagnosis of cancer. Then for a while I tried to follow up on her, but every time I saw her, she'd be like thanks a lot, I don't really need to talk right now, but when I need to talk I'll let you know. And then I got a call from her daughter saying my mom is here, she will not get out of her bed, she is completely berserk with fear, and sadness, blah, blah, blah. I went and made a home visit. I went to this woman's house, and sat on her couch. She said to me, I should have talked with you. I was really upset. Every time I saw you, you were like the cancer man. And everyone here is going to make me talk about cancer. So I just brushed you away because that meant I didn't have to talk to the cancer man. I said that's okay. And so we did talk. And, you know she did end up dying, but at least she could break out of this thing. You know it was an interesting projection. Usually the cancer patients think of themselves as being the cancer man or cancer woman. But for her, the professional who wanted to talk to her about her feelings was the cancer man. It was like I had the disease. Or not that I had it, but I controlled it, compelled it and if she could remove contact with me everything would be fine.

From what I can see, I think doctors, like I said, they may say in their heart of hearts I failed to keep the patient alive, but in the literature they say the patient failed to respond to such and such. So again, yes, a veiled attempt of denial associated with death. Um huh, doctors don't want to take responsibility because that would shatter their own illusions. I had a patient in one of the groups and she said, something to the effect, that she was asking a doctor how long am I gonna live? He said, well, two months ago I told you had six months to live. That's two months minus two is four, so I guess you've got four months. (laughs). And I think as a way of saying "f___ you" she was in the group three and a half years later.

Oh yeah, the psychological impact is devastating. And some people will live as long as either they are told to or as long as they have programmed themselves to. Even support groups themselves, the literature says that women with breast cancer who are in breast cancer support groups outlive those who are not in support groups. And my own experience is certainly that most of the people who were in the support group were already past their time, or who were within the process of being in the group went past their time. I remember one time we even had a bottle of champagne with this woman because she was supposed to have been dead two years ago on this date. To give credit, many of the doctors that I deal with now will not give a date unless we say to them the family wants this patient to be in a hospice program. For the hospice criteria they have to have prognosis of six months or less. A lot of doctors now, I think, are starting to shy away from that, or giving it in global terms, but a lot doctors aren't.

Mark: When do the doctors let go? When do they let go and stop the chemotherapy and all these treatments?

This is a situation where myself and the nurses sometimes do get involved. Like I said, there are times in which we are more or less supporting, counseling the doctors to allow this to happen. Oh yes, it does go on a lot. From what I could see, I would say yes, that more treatment is used than necessary. I would say that almost every patient that I have seen who is in end-stage cancer has received over treatment in some variety. You see what they do in bad cases. I mean after all, this guy has a brain tumor and it's giving him terrible headaches and he's gonna die anyway, then a little radiation. I don't know if I would call that over treatment, but certainly as far as like I said with the feedings, which in any hospice or terminal care facility is considered to be aggressive treatment. That's a very hard thing to let go. I guess that's hard because then, what are you doing? Are you starving the patient? It feels then more like they're killing someone if they don't even do these things, that is what is hard to understand. Doctors who deny the death also often times deny the pain, the physical pain of the patient. The actual physical pain. Emotional pain, yes, but I'm talking now about the physical pain. I have seen many doctors say, "Oh, no, you know you can't, you know, give them Tylenol III. I can't put them on morphine; they'll get addicted. Someone has to say how are they gonna be addicted? And studies show that about 4 percent of people who are given narcotic painkillers become addicted, and pretty much had a history of addiction.

They're doing this, no, obviously if your prescribing morphine then someone is going to get paid for it. It might be, but I think it's more, I think it's more of a puritan kind of "Well, you've got cancer, so what's a little pain?" They don't say that, but that's the underlying thing. They could be driving up the bill. I know that, that goes on. And I know that there have been cases that people have felt what is the chemo for? I think we won't know those cases clearly until this whole denial of death thing is worked out, which of course, that's like, you know, that's infinity. You can never quite get there. I mean we all nod our heads and say, "Oh yes, you were trying to keep the patient alive." Of course, you get paid more for treating more, but I think that it's more a "No, no, this guy's not gonna die, than getting paid." But who knows?

We are a Medicaid receiving hospital, and we're a 911 receiving hospital, so folks of all colors and classes come here. People oftentimes without any insurance, poor people with Medicaid. Generally, my experience has been that patients, who have Medicaid or have no coverage, tend to be minorities and tend to get second class treatment. For example, this is a teaching hospital, so doctors are on rounds. Usually those covered by the medical service, these poor patients that I'm talking about, are the ones who will wake up in the morning and will find six doctors looking at them and poking them and basically using them as a living biology experiment. It is dehumanizing. And, as a matter of fact I have, quite a few times, gotten involved with getting patients exempt from that. Working in a hospital is very, very difficult for a caring person because they are here to basically increase the revenues of the hospital. Some places are harder than others, and we cope with it by making jokes, and we refer to our jobs sometimes as flipping hamburgers because the patients are supposed to come in, they're supposed to get out. They're called DRG (Diagnostic Related Groups), which is quite extraordinary, because sometimes, I'll get from people, "Wait a minute, my fathers dying. Why does he have to get out of the hospital at a certain point?" And then I'm in a situation in which I have to explain to them the logic of the hospital, "other patients need the bed so that they can get treatment and you know, everything is being done for your father." I put in a very nice way, of course, but they see I'm saying get your father out of here so we can bring in another patient. And it's kind of a schizophrenic or disassociate thing that I have to do. There are times I can be myself and there are times in which I have to be representative of the hospital, and I say, "Look, I'm sorry but the bottom line is the bottom line."

It's been very interesting for these last three years because, well, you know, just . . . you're at a party and someone says, "What do you do?" And I say, "I'm an oncology social worker." Oncology? What's that? Cancer. Wow, how depressing. (laughs). Just when I say I deal with cancer people, someone will say to me, "God that's so depressing." And I will find oftentimes that I have to say to them, "No, it's not." But it depends on the person. Or else I'll say, "Yeah, but there's always being a key puncher." I think the reality is that if you're in social work there isn't a happy, perky social work field. It's either child abuse, drug abuse, AIDS, homeless or, let's face it social work is not a happy-go-lucky field, anyway.

The draw? Well, I think part of it was like I said the spiritual part. Part of it could be the whole family thing, you know, the history in my family, and trying to tie together some loose ends from that. I don't know. I mean, what the heck, I'm training to be a psychotherapist, so of course I'm going to look at it that way. The reward is just being a regular psychotherapist. As a social worker you have to deal with a lot of bullshit, especially if you're going to be seeing people on an ongoing basis. They can play games with you for eight months, and your happy because you're getting paid for each session. But if you're faced with people that are either dying or a family member is dying, then you're stripping a lot of bullshit away, and you're talking person to person, and you're dealing with the ultimate question. It's just an amazing thing to be part of. There was this old guy, he was 82, and his family was falling apart. He was the pillar of strength for the family. And they were like, "Oh, my God you can't go, blah, blah, blah . . ." Meanwhile, he's sitting there on his bed, and he's saying, "God is a loving God. And it's too bad about my family, but they should never put that much faith in one human being.

That's not what I am. I'm just one person, and I'm happy and I'm ready."
And I was only on the job for two weeks, and I said to myself, "Holy shit."

*   *   *

Jeff was an earnest person very willing to talk about his new job as an oncology social worker. Similar to Cindy, he pulled no punches when speaking about how others managed life after being diagnosed with cancer; how he coped working with terminally ill patients and the communicative process between social workers, doctors, patients and their families.

Jeff no longer works at the hospital where I met him. I have been unable to locate him.

CHAPTER 2

Nurses

MARCY

What gets me up every day is my curiosity of the process of life, and the process of death, which is part of life. Each person does it uniquely as they experience the melody of their whole lives. Each is as individual as a set of fingerprints. And I learn something from each death. There is something there for me: tremendous satisfaction. My patients have taught me to live one day at a time, and this has helped me to survive many things. My patients teach me how to cope, minute by minute. They teach me about laughter. Some patients have given me the gift of laughter. Some of them give me love, the purest, most unconditional love, which is very moving. It's not the man-woman kind of love. It's sort of being to being. It's that simple, and it's wonderful to be able to experience the essence of that in the nurse-patient relationship.

For the past nine years I've been a hospice nurse. My specialty is symptom management and to prepare for the inevitable event of death. This is also the job of social workers, but I'm involved as well. If people will let me in just a little bit, I can build that bridge of trust at the first meeting. I am passionately committed to their feelings and to helping the patient understand what's going on in their body. I do this for the family as well. To establish trust I talk a lot with the patient. I tell them stories, true stories, of my experiences in life. I've been ill many times myself, gravely ill, so I have a personal store of experiences to draw on. Sometimes I make up stories, using metaphors from literature or poetry.

I have a patient who is dying of cancer that has metastasized all over. We thought he would die over the weekend. I said good-bye; everyone was prepared. In this family the son is a physician, his wife is very with it, the daughter is a nurse, and they're all very involved in his care. But he's suddenly going through some very exotic transformation. I medicated him when I went to visit him today and his rabbi was there. He had not told the rabbi how ill he was. We changed his medication and

I suggested he lie down and let it take over, to daydream a little bit. I said, "Just go with the flow. Feel your pain then feel the medication taking it away. Perhaps a little bit of music might be helpful." His wife brought the radio in then left.

What struck me was that this man, who is 70 years old, a mechanical engineer who's always been staid, is listening to rap music! He's lying in bed snapping his fingers to the beat of rap music. He's more than interested in this form of music; he suddenly has a craving for it. This led us to a discussion of what might have prompted this sudden craving. Perhaps he was getting ready for his next reincarnation, I suggested. This is not a man who's into new age stuff and I'm not either, usually, and if I were, he'd hardly be someone with whom I would discuss reincarnation, but it just sort of naturally flowed. We talked for about half an hour then he fell asleep, still listening to rap.

I take what's happening in a patient's life at a given moment, in terms of what he or she is feeling and I try to use it, as when we started talking very boldly about reincarnation. Sometimes I believe in it; sometimes I don't. It depends on the time and place. I change, too.

In fact it's all about change. Death is really the only thing I haven't done. I've done everything else. I've had babies; I've been in love. I've changed in many ways. Now my next change, besides growing older, is into death. It's a kind of cocoon; a kind of metamorphosis that is very acceptable. I have tremendous curiosity about what this change process is, and I want to be helpful in facilitating this change in others so that I may learn how to better change for myself. I often feel I want to mother the patients by keeping them cozy and warm and bathed, lying on clean sheets. One of my territories was in the South Bronx where clean sheets weren't always available, and I would even bring sheets from home. But it finally dawned on me that not everyone has the clean, white deathbed syndrome. This was my need, not the patients'. So that was another change in me. It's just sort of one big symphony of change.

Sometimes I actually witness the dying process itself. It's very peaceful. Remember those old-fashioned lights on a string? Switches on a string? It's exactly like that. It's as if someone pulled the string and turned off the lights. Remember that these are planned deaths. I'm not talking about violent deaths or anything like that. I'm talking about death in a hospice environment where, hopefully, the patients and families have been prepared.

The way I got into hospice nursing was kind of a fluke. We were living upstate and my husband died. We moved back to New York and I had to earn a living to support my kids. Someone told me a new hospice was opening in the Bronx and I did a hospice there. It felt so right because I'm very committed to people where it has to do with their dying and a lot of their feelings. At one point in this early period of my hospice career I acquired a patient who I could see was very close to death. The home health attendant had to leave and there was a gap of an hour between when the woman's daughter came home and when the attendant left. So I felt I couldn't leave this woman. She was also in considerable pain and distress, grieving distress. I gave her morphine, which was the prescribed drug, and she died. I was okay. I did what I had to do. I called the daughter. Everything was cool.

I went home and took my walk. And then I remember breaking a set of Baccarat flutes. I broke every single one of them in the fireplace, because suddenly it dawned on me that not only was I an agent for change and for comfort, but perhaps I had killed this person. Everyone in hospice goes through this. I'm sure doctors do, too. Giving her morphine to ease her pain was perhaps the thing that stopped her. I called the doctor at home and asked to meet with her to discuss what I was feeling. I felt that I had taken control where I should have allowed the patient to take control. But I began to realize that I hadn't killed the patient. I had not pushed her over the edge. She would have died anyway. Perhaps I made her death a little bit more comfortable, but I did not personally kill her. That was my first experience where I was alone with the patient, had given the medication, and the patient died. This has happened several times since.

There is still controversy about medication for cancer patients. Some argue it doesn't necessarily prolong life as much as it prolongs death. People are surviving longer for whatever reasons. They need to survive, perhaps. Cancer of the cervix can be cured now, but breast cancer is no different now than it was 40 years ago. Worse perhaps. So, in spite of all the treatments, people just die. And from my perspective, what they're prolonging is not so wonderful. Perhaps for them, because it's their life, it's necessary to prolong it, but the manner in which they're living is awful.

There's a kind of arrogance that healthcare people have, and I deliberately call it arrogance. We sometimes feel, and I used to feel this way, that our patients can't survive without us. But it's not true. People survived perfectly well before I came on the scene and would, indeed, survive perfectly well if I weren't there. Possibly even better, because I may have messed something up in her continuum.

The basic function of a hospice, and they have been around for centuries in one form or another, is to support the dying patient and the family in the last part of the patient's life and into a comfortable, non-threatening death. Most medical doctors are not supportive of hospices. If they were, we'd have two floors in this large hospital instead of only eight beds. Doctors are still not taught that death is a normal phenomenon. It's not even a phenomenon, but a normal part of life. Just as normal as birth. Doctors are still taught that death is something they've got to fight with everything in their arsenal. They have not come to terms with death, so how can they counsel a patient? When there's nothing else to be done I believe it is best to place a patient in a supportive, therapeutic environment. We don't exclude the primary doctor; we work with them when the patient comes to us. I think the denial of death, the repression of death, is particularly an American/ Western cultural thing. It's part of our youth culture, where 65-year-old ladies are having face-lifts to try to be 18 again. All that stuff is denial of the aging process. A denial of what really inevitably comes.

I think there is a basic lack of communication between the physician and the patient. Perhaps one-fifth of the time, on the referral form, the physician will check off that s/he has *not* discussed DNR, which means, "do not resuscitate," with the patient. The patient does not know what the prognosis is. And these are oncologists, mind you. They do not wish to remain the patient's physician and prefer the hospice medical director take to the patient's care. What they're saying is that they did everything they could but can't cope with the rest. Nor do they want to. I pity the physician in such cases because they've been trained to preserve life at all costs. It must be a very deflating and empty feeling when they fail. And it's a process in which they're going to fail each time, because we all die.

I would like to see physicians become comfortable helping their patients deal with dying. There are very few cures for major cancers. There are postponements, perhaps, and so-called remissions. Then about five years down the road metastasis happens. Perhaps this brings up the question, not necessarily of euthanasia, but of suicide. I would like doctors to be comfortable with helping their patients do that. If the physician has really given everything in terms of supporting the patient on the road to death and the patient says, "Okay, I've had enough physical and emotional suffering," the doctor could respond, "Okay, I'll go with you the last step." They could do it together. Don't forget the physician has replaced the high priest, the shaman, in our culture.

In talking to doctors, I frequently suggest symptom management because, oddly enough, most oncologists don't know very much about pain management. They are not heavily into narcotic pain management and don't want to deal with it. Even though pain is always brought up in these discussions, they're very unskilled in managing it. They don't really get into it because they're not there to see the pain. When doctors are making rounds, they're in and out. They don't see and don't experience the pain. Pain is not just a result of the disease state; it's also from the mental state. Social and cultural issues come out in a person's life which create other kinds of pain, and physicians don't recognize that.

When doctors read about Dr. Jack Kevorkian, they may mentally pat him on the back, but they can't do a damn thing about it because they haven't faced issues of dying within themselves. As a body they could change this whole attitude very easily so it wouldn't have to be changed state by state. Doctors could simply come out and say, "Hey, this is a natural thing. This is normal. We all die. Whether we die at 99 or at 49, we all die. We all have to move and make room. That's the way the life cycle works. And it's okay. It's really okay."

I think training doctors to communicate with patients should start early, in the first semester of medical school. One local medical school now encourages students in their fourth year to rotate in a hospice program. Actually, I feel that medical students should be trained together with nursing students, by taking one course a week or one course a month, on death and dying. Or on living. A course called "Life." It may sound corny, but is think it would be marvelous because it would teach doctors that nurses are equal to them in what they do, and that it's okay to communicate openly, rather than from a hierarchical standpoint.

A myth that needs to be dispelled is that death is a frightening, final thing. It's not. It doesn't hurt. There's a kind of peaceful look right around the very end and that is the body's way of making itself comfortable, to cease being in this world. It's something people should be aware of and not scared about. In a sense, I feel really offended and righteously indignant that people are afraid of dying. They have accepted that it's okay to be born. Now it's okay for small children to witness a birth. Why shouldn't it be okay for small children to witness a death?

I have a patient who at the present has two sets of grandchildren, a set of two and a half year-old twins by the daughter who's a nurse, and one five-year-old grandchild by the son, who's a physician. In a discussion I had with the family, I encouraged the parents to allow the children to visit their grandfather. The daughter responded favorably and brought her children to visit. The son, after a consultation with a psychiatrist, said no, absolutely not, that the children would be traumatized forever. They must not see this man die. This goes back to the attitudes of doctors, where there's still that myth about death being a scary, awful, traumatizing thing and it's not. It's not.

Fortunately the Surgeon General is on the right track. She has come out with the declaration that teaching kids about life in general, and about health, should begin in kindergarten. It's a good time to talk about death as well, and to program the new generation that this is all normal; it's part of life. Education is the key.

In a way, part of me is the same person and part isn't, since working as a hospice nurse. I've had to change and do a lot of work. I would say the vast majority of people who do hospice work, in the beginning can't separate themselves from their patients and their problems, and somewhere along the way they really burn out. And when they do, they either get out of hospice work or they realize they need help to let go of some of this stuff. I have to celebrate who I really am, the whole of me. Not just the hospice nurse of me, because I'm other things, too. I'm a woman. I'm a mother. I'm a friend. Not only a nurse, although I'm also a very good nurse, as it happens. You're a lot of things. You're a human being. You have a lot of traits you have to feel comfortable with. For me, basically, if you love somebody unconditionally, you let them go. Because you realize they don't need you. So we're not talking about death as much as we're talking about how you live your life.

Some patients and family members, from my experience, get it together to deal with the issues, but some don't. Some go kicking and screaming. Everyone in my experience who has ever faced death knows they're going to die. Small children do. A two-year-old child with acute leukemia said to me, "I'm going on God's choo-choo train tonight and I'm not coming back." And sure enough the kid died that night. So I think it's given, probably to all living things, to know when the end is coming.

One of the things I can give to other people is a sort of living testament that it's possible to survive, and survive fairly well. In spite of basically being a cynic, I still find the work that I do life affirming. I have survived an incredible number of losses since I was little girl, but all in all, I've done quite well. And doing this kind of work is very life affirming because I see other people surviving their losses, too. Other people are surviving losses much greater than mine. The life affirming thing about it is I think it's really a rehearsal for my own death. All this that I am doing is learning how to die, in case of being caught unaware here, or on my way home, or wherever, so that I do it gracefully.

I don't know if there's a balancer out there who's balancing all those wonderful things. These mitzvahs that I give, so when my turn comes, and I'm lying in some bed in Calcutta, someone will come and lift me up and put me in this clean, white deathbed that I fantasize about. As much as I'd like someone to be there, I just don't know if there will be. That's where the cynicism comes in. I hope that, having done this so many times and having witnessed so many people in life and so on, that I will be able to do it for myself. I will not need anyone to do it for me. *I* will be able to do it for me.

I once thought I would like to be a midwife, assisting my husband in his obstetrics practice, but I can't imagine not doing hospice. Perhaps in the country somewhere. Perhaps in England. I'd really like to try it in England, or in Cornwall or Wales. Even Scotland, to see how another culture is accepting of this form of dealing with the end. But definitely in a rural practice, wherever that might be.

Above all, be honest with yourself. Be very scrupulous and honest. If you're hurting, get help. If you're happy, share it with your patients, with your colleagues. And support. Just be open, as open as you can. Support is very important. Not necessarily from the therapist but also from groups. The family. A group of friends. But preferably from a professional group because they are more likely to understand your pain or your discomfort, or your puzzlement, or whatever is going on. Hospice is not for everyone. You really have to feel the joy and stop to smell the flowers. Do good things for yourself. That's very important.

*   *   *

"Benign cynic" is how Marcy is described in my field notes. Beneath the innocuous cynicism was one of the most giving and caring individuals I had the fortune of meeting. Marcy's vivid, metaphoric recollections of life inside and outside the hospice made her a truly complex, three-dimensional personality to talk with and learn from.

I saw Marcy over dinner in 1998, around Christmas, seven years after our interview. We had a wonderful time catching up. She was working for some medical insurance company. She had left hospice care four years earlier due to a falling out with management. She disliked her new job and was thinking of going outside New York to find hospice work. Marcy's faced beamed with pride when I mentioned that her interview was one of two the publishers enjoyed enough to offer me a contract. Before entering a cab to go home, she wished me a happy holiday, and success with the book, which she always thought a good idea. We made plans to meet again after New Years. As the cab pulled away Marcy turned smiling, and waving through the back window. I waved back. It was the last time I saw Marcy.

Marcy died two weeks after New Years Eve in 1999. She had been found alone, dead in her apartment on the bathroom floor of unknown causes. Marcy had told me that being a hospice nurse was really a rehearsal for her own death. With all the "mitzvahs" she performed she had hoped her death would be a graceful one. I doubt that occurred, but I would like to believe someone lifted her up and put her in the "clean, white death-bed" she wished for upon dying.

DAN

John Dunne wrote in "No Man Is an Island" that "each man's death diminishes me." I believe this is true. I think for myself that I have sort of built in some sort of mechanism that allows me to get involved all the way. I mean some people will pull back. People laugh at me because I make it sound religious by saying I was called to this job. I was called to this. I was chosen to deal with people who are dying, and it makes me sad. It makes me sad for a while. But my strength comes back to me.

I'm what they call a Staff Level II nurse. Half the time I take care of seven to eight patients a day, and half of the time, the other days, I'm in charge of about 35 patients and supervise the nurses on the floor who are taking care of those patients. I see mostly cancer patients and people receiving chemotherapy or radiation treatment. We occasionally get an HIV patient with Kaposi's Sarcoma. We used to get all different types of HIV patients, but now we just get KS patients who receive chemo.

I've been doing this for 10 years. This is a second profession for me. I used to work on computers at a bank, which I also did for about 10 years. I never liked it, and they were encouraging me to go to school, so I thought if I had to go to school I should do something I wanted to do. And for some reason I always wanted to be a nurse, and everyone thought I was crazy, because at that time I was making a very, very nice salary, and the starting salaries for nurses were not very good. However, salaries are a lot better now.

I always wanted to be a nurse, and it was something I always did. Growing up I had a sickly grandmother and I was one of 10 grandchildren and I was sent to take care of her. I did it and I liked doing it. I always found myself doing things for sick people in the neighborhood. I started by doing they're shopping for them, them I took care of a paraplegic for two years, which involved bathing and lots of things like that.

It's very important in nursing practice to try to help someone, and not to judge and label people. You have to look at the whole person and try to empathize with them. It's very important to convey this non-judgmental acceptance, especially when talking about HIV patients. People are very uneducated to begin with about the background of patients. At first this was typically a "gay" disease, and most of your population here is not gay, so they don't really know anything about gay life, and people were afraid. Some people didn't accept, you now. And it was important to show that gay people were people. Before they were gay people they were just people and they were sick people, and they had to be helped. And in the early days I saw some terrible things where people wouldn't go into a room, or were very short with a patient, and I found that very upsetting. But it's changed. It's a lot better.

I worry about my own death and that nobody will be there for me. Supposedly if you give you get back. I don't know if that's necessarily true. One hopes that it is. One hopes that it's not all in vain what one's doing. I have a terrible fear of dying alone. I hope there will be somebody compassionate there to help me out. I don't care if it's a nurse, but I hope there will be some caregiver around me who is really nice. I mean, I make my patients feel good. Whether I'm making a joke about myself, or whatever, or just sitting holding them, but I have that knack. And that's what people need when they're dying. There's no time for lectures no time for false hope. It's just somebody there, accepting. And that's why I got into oncology nursing. That's why I chose this particular field. I knew there were no cures. I don't think you'll ever hear anyone say that—that they came into to help people die. But again, honestly, I'm getting in touch with myself because I'm terrified, terrified. It started in my childhood and I haven't outgrown it. I've had people to say to me, "How can you be around all those dying people?" It's actually quite easy. If you get in touch with that in yourself, it's very easy to take care of these people.

I have friends who don't understand why I'm doing this; have no idea why I'm doing this. And when I explain it they still don't understand. This is very uncomfortable for some people, to get in touch with that part of themselves. It's usually done very privately and it takes people a long time, if ever, to get in touch with that part of themselves, which could be your soul, I don't know. That's interesting, to talk about someone's soul, isn't it? Each death diminishes you, and this job takes a piece of your soul, every day. And the soul is very hard to replace. That hurts; that hurts terribly.

I find that doctors often, as the patient progresses in their terminal illness, maybe in the last two weeks, will really, quite honestly, get lost. I don't find that much with the nurses. They seem to stick around right to the end. But it's very hard to find a doctor, the attending doctor anyway, in the last two or three weeks of a patient's life that he's taken care of for a year or two.

It would help very much if medical schools would assign students to dying patients, but they don't like to do that. We don't get students on our floor until they're just ready to graduate because they think our floor is too tough. And when I say too tough, is that because we have so many IV's, and they said to me, "No, it's because too many people are dying and they're not ready for it." Well I don't know when they're gonna be ready for it, because this is what happens in a hospital.

There's a very famous attending doctor at this hospital who probably brings in more oncology patients than anyone else in the whole hospital, and he never speaks to his patients. Most of his patients, a lot of his patients, believe it or not, you'll find it written somewhere in the chart, "patient doesn't know diagnosis . . . do not speak to patient . . . do not mention word 'cancer' . . ." Can you believe this is 1992? Thank God they're not all like this. But this is a very important doctor here, and very good, mind you. But it does put the caregiver in a very funny place because you're dealing with terminal illness, and then to have someone say, "well, they don't really know what you have." Most of the doctors now are very compassionate and will talk with them. And some are frightfully honest and will say, "You know the chemo doesn't work anymore. Maybe you'll have two or three months. Why don't you go on a trip."

I remember a patient who had been through chemo and it worked for two years. Then it started to fail and he wanted some answers. The doctor told him it didn't look good. He didn't say, "You'll be dead in three months," he said "It doesn't look good." The patient pushed for a time period. And he said, "If all things went wrong, we'd say maybe three or four months." This patient got himself together and went to the South of France. This isn't going to work for everyone, but when this patient came back he was so happy because it was the one thing he had wanted to do in his life. And he said he might not have had the chutzpah to get himself together and tell his wife or whoever that it was time to go do that. He was well enough to enjoy it and he was there for about six weeks. He came home for two more weeks, then died in a week. And in that week he told me he was very glad the doctor told him, because for him it worked. I had an aunt who was diagnosed with lymphoma, and she was the sweetest, most wonderful woman you'd ever want to meet. And she was diagnosed rather late, I mean she was 84. She became a monster. You never saw such a personality change in your life. I mean she really became a monster. She was unbearable to live with.

You have to take your cues from the patient. I've had patients that want you to sit on their bed and hold them and cry with them. You do it. I have patients who don't want to speak. So you don't speak that day. But you get so you know, and you clarify with the patient, "Is this what you want?" And usually, especially with AIDS patients, they seem to die emotionally quite differently from cancer patients, which is interesting.

They don't seem to be as angry. *As* angry. Although some often are. I wonder if a lot of it has to do with the treatment. We (nurses) have talked about this a lot, the fact that right now, unfortunately, you get HIV or you have full-blown AIDS, it's a death sentence. There's nothing that's going to cure it. However, you get these cancer patients and you have your doctor saying, "Well now this chemo might work . . ." especially a female with breast cancer, which now today they say if caught early is practically curable. So you get these patients who are very edgy because they're wondering, "Am I going to be cured?" They tend to be a little more difficult to take care of than AIDS patients. I think most AIDS patients I've taken care of have made their peace. But the cancer patients are always hanging in there, hoping the chemo's going to work, hoping the radiation's going to work, you know? They're a little angrier, I think, on a daily basis. The family is very angry, too. The family is very affected by the diagnosis. I find them more angry with cancer than they are with AIDS. In the last two years I've seen more people staying around with the HIV patients. But it depends. It depends on how someone's dying. You know, some people die very hard. We're talking vomiting blood every day. I'm talking being transfused and then sitting on a bedpan and having blood come out, and being very alert until the end. People tend to run away from that. And now if someone becomes comatose, which is a nice death, to go to sleep and not wake up, families tend to stay around for that. That to me is an easy death. If you just go to sleep, that's sort of easy.

Families are afraid. They don't know what to say to the patient. Somebody's dying and they're spitting up blood, you know, they don't know what to say to them to calm them, arouse them. And they get hysterical themselves.

It's very hard to get nurses on a steady basis on this unit. We have lot of turnover. We only have two or three nurses who have been here more than ten years. The longest people tend to stay is a year and a half or two years, because people fear death. Working here forces people to confront their own mortality. There's also a technical side to this whole nursing business, too. Besides dealing with the emotions and accepting death, whether you're holding someone and allowing them to speak, or to cry, it's also a very heavy technical day of mixing antibiotics and of doing this and that. When you're breaking your back physically, and then you have something emotional that's crossing over, it's very heavy, it's tiring, it's exhausting, and people don't necessarily want to stay around and do this. In this particular institution there is a nurse who comes in once a week to run a support group. People attend, but you've got to understand, there are teeth in that gift of allowing you to vent your feelings. It's done on our time, and again, we have very hectic schedules, so you're asked to come in off the floor between 11:30 and 12:30, one of the busiest times of the day. Those who come in and want to get things off their chests are so worried about that hour they're going to lose because they know something may happen, something may be forgotten. While it's very nice for the hospital to say it offers this, we don't really have the time to stop a whole hour in a day. And to really unload emotionally, to just come at 11:30 and say "Go" and "This is the way I feel, and this happened, and so-and-so died, and it made me feel bad . . ." I find it doesn't work. it doesn't work for me. I've stopped going. I did it privately because I didn't want to influence anyone in the group by saying I wouldn't go. I just stopped going and I told the moderator, "I can't really focus on getting in touch with my feelings when I'm worried about what's going on out on the floor. I've got so many antibiotics to hang, and this has to be done, that has to be done, that so-and-so may fall out of bed . . ." So it doesn't work for me. But they do offer a weekly support group. I think a lot more should be done for physicians and nurses, as far as support is concerned with these issues.

One does need an outlet outside the hospital to get rid of all this. I have a couple of very good friends who are almost like a support group, who don't mind sitting and having a beer and talking about these kinds of things. I mean most people would think you're crazy and say, "Listen, I don't want to have a beer with this guy. He's gonna talk about death and dying. or he's gonna talk about his deep down inside feelings." This isn't what we talk about when we have a beer. But I'm lucky enough to have two friends like that. I could have more. I think I need more exercise to physically let the stress out, because it's very stressful. Very stressful. I think it affects your performance, the emotional side of your performance, the given side, the important side. I mean you can keep things in and still manage to handle your seven patients and take your vital signs and administer your medications, but you're certainly not going to be very effective communicating. If you're holding something in, say if Mr. X died last week and it really upset you, and you haven't let it go, and you have no outlets, then you can't let anything else in. So then the seven current patients are out of luck. It's very important to let it out and some people don't, and yes, their performance is affected. We very rarely address the emotional side of our work. I very rarely hear it. And not only here, anywhere I go. When I speak with other nurses, when we start talking about work, the last thing we ever touch on is the emotional side of the work.

A few years back we had a nurse called a Supportive Care Nurse who we were able to call if a patient or family member was having a difficult time. She just worked with our floor, and she wasn't called every day, so she could spend two hours a day with a patient, holding their hands and help them get through the grieving process. That was very beneficial because some of these people do need one-on-one help, and the doctor can't always be there, and neither can the nurse. This was a very good idea. I don't know whether it was because of finances or what, but they did away with that position. Maybe they should make me the Supportive Care Nurse; that's actually the part I like to do. I get very annoyed that I'm spending two hours mixing antibiotics. I'd rather be out there holding someone's hand or stoking him or her emotionally, you know, to help them have a better day.

I have gone to meeting after meeting here, and when they talk about staffing I have said that no nurse here should have more than four patients, and they laugh at me. And I've also spoken about the special needs of oncology patients, and of the HIV patients, and those special needs coming mostly from the psychosocial side and emotional sides of the issue. You see, a lot of times when we talk about being short staffed, the point is for these dying people, it's all emotional, and that's takes a lot of time. It takes a lot of time because you have to make yourself comfortable. You don't just go in and say, "Listen, I'm here to make you feel better emotionally." It takes time to establish that relationship that trusts. And it doesn't happen when you say, "Oh, I'm sorry, I've got to go now because so-and-so is calling me."

I find it interesting what impression people have of a good nurse. For example, there was a nurse on our floor a few years ago who was always done on time and everyone thought she was the greatest; the doctors thought she was great. She was a beautiful young lady; however, she never spoke to her patients. Never. Never ever. Except, "Good morning, my name is . . . pills pills pills." She never asked them anything about what they were feeling, but many people complimented her. That's always interested me, and I still see it to this day. It's very interesting what people think is a good nurse. And on the flip side, I remember one night when I had a very bad day because I had taken so much in emotionally from several patients, and I was leaving here two hours late, and someone commented I must have been very disorganized that day. But I realized it was because I did so much more.

*   *   *

For Dan nursing was a calling. By treating dying patients with respect and dignity he hoped would be cared for in similar fashion when his time came. Such an admission underscores a deep- rooted reason for working with terminally ill people. Like Marcy, he also speaks in metaphoric and spiritual terms when recounting such thoughts and feelings.

This type of communication or language provided Dan, as well as Marcy, with a positive self-identity, professional purpose, and way to effectively cope with the constant loss of life seen everyday.

I have been unable to find Dan. He left the hospital where he worked several years ago.

VICKY

I'm a clinical nurse specialist in neuro-oncology and orthopedic oncology. The orthopedic part I've been doing for a year and I've been in neurology for twelve years. When I was in nursing school I thought I wanted to be a psyche nurse, but I attended a baccalaureate program so when we graduated we all thought we didn't have the skills. I wanted to get the skills so I knew I needed to go someplace where I could get them and continue to use my psychiatric skills as well. Oncology seemed like a good blend of the two. So I went to work here on an oncology research unit and never looked back. I never went into psychiatry, although I did get my masters in psychiatric nursing. But I never wanted to work an inpatient psyche unit again. I just loved doing oncology.

Working in oncology epitomizes what being a nurse is. There's a sense of intimacy that nurses have with their patients that I don't think any other professional has. When I went into family therapy training I realized I was the only nurse in the program. The rest of the people were social workers. As a nurse I wanted to give people hugs. I wanted to be intimate and immediate with them, in a way my other colleagues, who were social workers, didn't seem to have a need for. It's just not their way of being in the world. As a nurse you're there 24 hours a day, seven days a week. That's our way of being in the world.

I want to learn new things and deal with equipment and all that kind of stuff, but then there is the other side, the feeling and thinking. As you're walking with a new patient down to their room, you're doing this checklist in your mind while you're doing their physical assessment and you're asking about terribly intimate things: their bowel patterns; their sexual habits; use of drugs. Very intimate things within the first half-hour of meeting them. But you're also wondering who is this person? And who is that with him? And how are they related? What's it like for them? It's their first admission. In oncology you're locked into the immediacy of life and death. For so many patients being diagnosed with cancer, no matter what type of cancer it is, I think they have this tremendous overload of feelings, emotions and anxieties that are associated with diagnosis. The most important thing in family counseling is to listen to the voices of the patients and families. Listening to the unspoken voice. Obviously you don't get attached or close to every patient you care for, and there are many patients who, if I didn't see them in a professional capacity, I'd never want to see them again. But there has been a series of patients, for whatever reasons, they strike a chord. They're kindred spirits. I see my function extending from period A to B. At period B my function in their lives is a natural end. I develop professional warmth, a professional relationship with them but I don't have a personal relationship with them that would endure for years. It's just that it's my professional relationship. There have been patients and families that I would have wanted to keep a relationship with, but for whatever reasons, it's difficult for them. It's very difficult for patient's families to come back here. They always say, "I'll come back." You never see them again. It's very unusual for families to come back.

I just had a patient's wife come back two weeks ago, very unusual. She's an unusual lady. She's Italian. This wonderful woman is very voluble, very down to earth, and real salt of the earth. I never knew her husband, except when he was demented from his brain tumor, so I don't know what he was like. But he was terribly disabled and she had young children when he was diagnosed. The youngest child was two, I think, when he was diagnosed. And then he was horribly disabled and had terrible hospitalization for many, many months. So I got to know her family quite well. I got to know her extended family quite well too because they were an extremely unusual bunch. She was a very strong woman and carried her family through it. She would survive and she's done quite well. She has a very dysfunctional family. Dysfunctional means having pathological relationships in the family. A family can't be dysfunctional before diagnosis. A general dysfunction will not allow them to survive the stress, the diagnosis and treatment. It's not just the normal life stresses; it's the chemotherapy that goes on for months and sometimes years; the continuous scans and follow-ups. And being followed here, I think, is extremely difficult too because you're not followed-up just by one service. There are many services. It's very hard for people to go back and resume their regular lives, even when they're on maintenance. So they have to be intact beforehand as a family member, or able to make the necessary changes to make the family function. This is very unusual during the period of diagnosis, treatment, and follow-ups.

The family has to readjust roles, whatever the tasks of the family are, whether it be raising their children or getting ready for retirement and death, and all those other issues. Very often these tasks have to be put on hold and that in and of itself can cause harm to the family unit. If you have young children at home, regardless of whether you're the wife or the husband, you still need to launch those children. That's the function of the family. But with all the stresses of the diagnosis and treatment, sometimes it's hard to see that still has to be done. You still have to attend to your children. Get them to school; make sure they're okay. Be the counselors and get them to the baseball games. Do all those other things. It's a tremendous strain, a tremendous strain. You're pre-morbid personality is exacerbated in this situation. That's all it is. And that goes for the whole family. People really struggle with it. They work hard at it. The priority has to be taking care of the ill person. It has to be. The people who do better at it are the ones with better social support and coping skills. The people who do worse at it are the ones who are socially isolated and have poor coping mechanisms to begin with. So there's a spectrum.

It's very important for the family to communicate but I think it has to be within the confines of what's socially acceptable for the people in that culture and also what's acceptable with that family framework. And again, it goes back to how that family functioned beforehand. I would not expect a family that had a lot of secrets and had poor boundaries to have a death scene as a norm between mother and child. That's not the way they ever worked before so they're probably not going to be able to do that now. But I think as a professional, you can provide an avenue for people to do that.

Physicians are essential to the communication process, but they aren't acculturated or educated enough to be facilitators. They're educated to be doers so they don't learn a lot of the skills in school. Nor are they given a lot of feedback from their colleagues. When they try to do things like that it's not approved of. It's unusual and it really stands out in your mind when you see a physician who has those skills. And I think it also has to with self-selection. Nurses don't become nurses by accident. Not in this day and age. People choose to become nurse because they want to, not because it's an okay thing for a woman to do. At one time women couldn't become doctors. They became nurses instead. That kind of stuff doesn't hold water anymore. I'm not a nurse by accident. I think it has to do with who you are. I was always a caregiver in my family and I think your mind behaves like that. You either put your skills to use in a healthy or an unhealthy way. Fortunately, for me, I can put it to use in a healthy way.

The whole hierarchy of how we administer care has changed. Nurses no longer see the healthcare team as a triangle, with the doctor at the top and nurse at the bottom. The doctors haven't caught up with that yet. They haven't been educated that way. The doctor does different things from what the nurse does and from what the physical therapist does, and from what the social worker does. And we all have a piece of the pie, the pie being the patient and the family. There's always going to be some overlap between what we do. We want to do good nursing, not bad medicine. So we're struggling with that issue, too. I see that there needs to be more of a compliment between what we do. We need to take the physicians off the top of the triangle and get them down in the real world with the rest of us, taking care of the patients as a team and listening to each other about what each of us knows intimately about the patient. It's about discussing the patient's treatment plan together as a group, and not just writing orders to be carried out. So I see it as complimentary. I don't see it as hierarchical.

People who choose to be nurses may have certain skills that enable them to do it more easily. Or they choose this profession because they think it's an area they can be the people they are. But I think we all have to study it; we all have to learn it. I can be as touchy feely as I want, but if I go in and fall apart and cry at the patient's bedside all the time it's not going to do them any good. So there are a lot of things nurses have to learn in order to keep pace with changing technology and there are a lot of things physicians have to learn to get them to the other side. The balance is tilted.

The physicians don't talk about their fears of mortality. They don't know what to do or what to say. There is a physician here who I like very much personally, but she had this habit of when patient's where dying of literally disappearing. Making herself unavailable. She wasn't a bad person. No one ever sat her down and said, "Look, this what I see." Doctors are uncomfortable acknowledging they feel sad. It also has to do with the fact that here we never say die. There's no such thing as an inoperable tumor here. We always operate. We do terrible things to people, terrible. But it's with the consent of the patient. We do things here they would never consider doing anywhere else. And that's why people come here. We very rarely reach a point where we say we can't do anything else for you. That's very hard and it's very rare that we say that to people. There is always something else we can do. I think it's pushing the envelope. You don't work here unless you want to be able to offer people this last thing. I do think there's a way to offer people the ultimate, the absolute ultimate in care but still allow them to have dignity and comfort as they're dying.

I took care of a young girl here almost two months ago, she's 21 years old, and she has sarcoma. She had this tumor she probably got from radiation treatment she had as an infant. She was developmentally disabled. She was retarded and disfigured. I can't speak about the quality of her life. Her family was not terribly available to her emotionally at this point. We sent her for a procedure where they amputate the leg right up to the hip, so you can imagine it. Like the whole hip is gone. It's very disfiguring. If you learn to walk later on you have this big heavy prosthesis that wraps around your waist and you have a leg. But she had very bad scoliosis. Her spine was really twisted. Her anatomy was abnormal. One day I went in to help her get ready for a procedure. She had been incontinent, so I took some sheets and am getting ready to clean her. I had no idea her anus had actually been pulled around and now was in the front, so that she would never be able to wear a prosthesis and would never be able to defecate in a sitting position. I tell you, that day was really bad. And it wasn't because of her developmental disability that I thought this procedure had not been worthwhile. Would I have wanted it? No. Did Dorothy? I don't know because I don't know that Dorothy had given her consent. But you see what I'm saying? Would I have wanted to have that procedure? It's hard to know because I'll tell you now, I have two small children and I would do almost anything to have a few more years with them. I have to give the surgeon credit. He thought he did the best thing for her.

As I've gotten older, especially since I'm married and have children, I want to make sure there's balance in my life between the work I do and my family, my home, my outside interests, and in taking care of me. I came to the realization that the world continues to turn without me. The job will get done. Many of the patients would still be here for the most part and that I needed to go home and regroup. Sometimes when I come in and see it's going to be a hard day, I say to people, "You know what, tonight we get to walk out of her." At the end of it I get to go home to my little house with my garden and my husband and my children. And the other part of it is I stop focusing on the fact that the patient has a brain tumor and is going to ultimately die. This focus shifts from the long-term pain trajectory of the patient's illness to more like, what can I do today to enhance this person's death? And for a nurse sometimes it's just a simple thing. I've had so many people tell me I'm the only one who gave them a bath that way. I'm the only nurse who made them feel comfortable doing their dressings. That I knew what I was doing and it gives them a sense of security. Just little things like that add immeasurably to a patient's quality of life. Particularly when you're in a hospital because they feel they're at the mercy of strangers. I think it's really important for people to feel they have somebody who's competent taking care of them. And for me competency doesn't mean that I have to know everything about their care but I have to have access to people who do. And so that's the message I give to people. Even if I don't know how to do something I'll find somebody who does. I will take care of you. I'll manage your care. I will make sure it gets done today. And these things add to a person's wellness, even when they are critically ill.

I certainly never avoid discussing a patient's illness and death with them. And I've also learned over the years when people ask me how long they have to live that nobody can really tell them. I've been fooled a lot of times. You'd think for sure they're going to be dead when you come in tomorrow, and they linger on for weeks or they go home. We've discharged people to terminal care facilities and they spent two years in a terminal care facility. I've been wrong so many times. I was sure somebody would die and they didn't. So now I tell people, "I don't know. Nobody can tell you. But today I want to make sure you're comfortable. I want to talk to you about how we're going to manage your care when you go home."

I am a different person now from when I graduated nursing school. I don't think I was idealistic. It's not that. I just think you see life differently. When you work with cancer patients you see how precarious life is. You immediately identify with all those people. You realize how fragile life is. I think it can make you a risk taker, in a very healthy sense. When you see people languishing on their deathbeds and they have a lot of regrets about things they didn't see, things they didn't do, you realize life is short. My husband reads boring books he's not enjoying. Life's too short to read books you don't enjoy. Get a book you enjoy.

I think cancer still has a lot of stigma for patients and for caregivers. The general feeling of the lay public when tell them you're a cancer nurse is, "Oh, how terrible." But in fact there are many cancers that are cured, curable, and treatable. Long periods of remission with good quality of life. And there are many cancers where we have made a lot of progress in 20 or 50 years. But there are still many patients who don't tell their employers they have cancer. They're still not able to purchase life insurance for certain diagnosis. They certainly have a hard time getting health insurance with a pre-existing condition like a cancer diagnosis even though you have a highly curable cancer like Hodgkin's disease or something like that. Those of us who work with it every day see the full spectrum of it, but I don't think the public does by any means. It's sad because patients come in with preconceived notions of what it is to get chemotherapy. They're all going to be sick as a dog and will lose all their hair. It doesn't work that way so the message we give to everybody is, "We're not going to treat you like a your friend Joe who had cancer and died. We're going to treat you like you. You're an individual and you have individual side effects. We're going to manage them and we'll take care of you." We really take it from the abstract, from Marcus Welby and General Hospital and bring it to each individual patient.

A nurse isn't what I do, it's what I am. It's who I am, so I don't live my life as anything other than a nurse. A nurse wherever I go. Whatever I do because that's my personality profile. I'm a caregiver. I make nice. I'm the one who wants to quiet everything down. Put a Band-Aid on the booboo. That's what I do. I can't imagine doing anything else. I never wanted to do anything else. When I was a little girl, I wanted to be a nurse. And as a matter of fact, I had an existential crisis when I was in nursing school because I never thought about doing anything else and when I was ready to graduate I thought, "Oh my God, what if I don't like it, what will I do with myself?" Really, I just found out I was one of those lucky few who always knew what I wanted. It really was my life's aspiration, vocation. And it's been as wonderful for me personally as I would ever have expected it to be.

*   *   *

Vicky impressed me with unflinching opinions, confidence, and commitment to her patients and profession. Vicky lived and breathed the role of nurse. She was the consummate professional, who was able to effectively balance a demanding work and family life. Her insights into the behavior and communication processes between nurses, doctors, dying patients, and their families provide readers with deeper knowledge of what the oncology world can be like.

Vicky left the hospital where we met just a few years after our interview. She is now teaching and practicing nursing in New Jersey, where she lives with her two children and husband, who is a respected medical oncologist. She is "loving every minute" of her new work environment.

This narrative was the second one Baywood Publishing Company liked enough to offer me a contract.

CHAPTER 3
Doctors

DR. WILLIAMS

There is always a patient that is going to have the most devastating disease. It is always a patient like that, you know, that brings you back. Gets you to say "Look at this. This is what I'm here for." I'm really here to make suffering less. You understand what I'm trying to say? You don't give up you don't say "Oh, my God this is terrible. I don't want to be around in that room." More than anything this makes the job gratifying for me. I've been a medical oncologist for ten, eleven years. I'm from Panama, in Central America and I studied medicine in Spain. I have been in the United States for twenty-three years. No, I didn't always want to be a doctor. I decided to become a doctor overnight. I was seventeen, in premed school, studying biology and parasitology. Both were new specialties at the University of Panama. They had us do three years of premed and then you went into one or two years of whatever interested you. So it was a new thing and a lot of people were going in it. And I always liked lab work. That I always liked. Everybody that was in premed school was going into medical school. Even the people who had gone to high school and never spoke of what they wanted to be. After I finished my second year of premed I went back home and all my friends were gone. I found out that everyone was going to medical school in Spain. The University of Panama had a contract with Spain because we didn't have enough doctors. Everyone was involved with this new medical program they had in Spain. After I found out about this I came home and said to my father, "I want to go to medical school in Spain." My father said, "You're crazy. You're a woman and women don't go to medical school. Men study something because they have to have a career and they get married and have kids." I didn't buy what my father said. I spoke with my mother and she said "If you really want to go think about it, and tomorrow we will talk." Tomorrow came and she asks me if I still want to go to Spain to study medicine. I said yes. So she spoke with my father and they looked into it. The medical program was well organized. Everyone was very young. One of my father's best friend's son was studying medicine in Spain. So my father knew everything. He said, "Look, I don't like it, you have a home, just write, and let me know if you ever want to come home. And I went, and I liked it and that was it.

I liked medical school. I was very good at diagnosing things. Before I gravitated to hematology and oncology I was planning on becoming a pathologist. I got accepted at St. Johns University for a pathology residency program. After a year, the chief resident of medicine said to me, "Listen, don't do pathology, this is not for you, you like to talk too much. It's a horrible thing to do. You're always in a room; you don't talk to people. Do medicine, you're young, you can always decide that you want to do something else." So I went into medicine. The first year I did internal medicine. The second year we had to do a rotation, and I wound up doing a rotation in hematology. In my fourth year I was chief resident. I could select any hospital to go do a rotation. I chose oncology. At the time I knew everything the fellows knew in hematology, but I didn't know much about oncology. All told, I did about two years of hematology and about six months or so of oncology. After my residency ended, I got two offers. One was to be the chief of a sickle cell program. The other was an oncology fellowship. I chose the oncology fellowship. Well, oncology is what you see most. You get more consults. Anemias are treated more by the internist, unless the patient really has a problem. I don't know if I'd enjoy it. Sometimes I don't know if I really enjoy oncology. I like to treat patients, see them do well, but that's, you know, not real. The patients don't do well. They don't do well.

What keeps me in it is that you make them feel a little better. I think that is one of the things that doctors should do. Doctors are supposed to be compassionate and nice, you know, warm, that kind of thing. I don't think that is really true, but these patients, in particular, need that kind of personality. I don't know if it is important, but I think they need to have that kind of personality or something like that. And then you couple that with some sort of hope. It's not the treatment; it's the hope. In certain Latin languages the word treatment means that you are not going to cure, but you are doing something to better the patient. But in English when you treat, you assume that you are going to get cured, and that is not true. The connotation is not the same.

I think many physicians—male and female—don't have the compassion to feel in this particular environment. I think it is very difficult. It's very difficult to be with people if they are dying and always giving of yourself. There comes a time when you just can't do anymore. It's difficult. You probably start out with all kinds of compassion, and then it's very emotional, and if you decide that you're going to shut it out you become very cold. Practicing medicine this way, for this group of people, shortchanges the doctor more so than the patient.

Because you look too much at yourself, not on how the patient is responding to you. If anything, you wonder if you're just not with it. I'm referring to going in every day and one patient comes in that can be easily handled and then you have a patient that you can't do anything for. The patient is looking for hope and help and you can't deliver. You sit there one hour with a patient and you can't give them any real hope. And you get into that patient's life and find out that the patient has unfinished business that cannot just disappear. And then your next fifteen patients come in with breast cancer. You understand? It's terrible. It's terrible.

You have good times. You have them when you get patients that have diseases that can be treated, and even if they have side effects you can treat it and the patient can go on and live. You can say that the book says that 50 to 80 percent of these patients are going to survive. It might be a rough road but we will be with you. Everybody is optimistic, so everything works out.

There is real hope for something like that, that there is not only hope there is some tangible evidence that these patients are going to do better. And you think that you're really doing something. So, in between all the bad times, there are certain good times that brighten the days. But, in general I think it is very depressing. It can be very depressing. I don't think it is guilt when you can't help these patients because we can't have guilt. It's not your fault. What you have is a feeling of incompetence. That's different. What do you call it when you—when there is nothing you can do? Helplessness? Helplessness. Sure. True, that's part of it. We do go through years of medical training where we have these ideals about saving people's lives and then we find out that we can't do it. I don't think that doctors behave as they do because they are looking at their own mortality or deny their own deaths. I don't think as a whole that that happens.

When I went into oncology they told us to get psychological testing, but I never went. It wasn't something important to me. I thought why would I need that. I can't explain it to you. I just thought it was not important. But some other people have gone through things and, you know, I've heard comments from them saying, "Oh my god, I cannot cope with bad, stressful situations." But I didn't know about this, because I didn't go. I just didn't do it. I thought that you only went to the psychologist or psychiatrist if something was really wrong with you. So, I didn't think something was wrong with me in the first place. But I really feel now that people should have some sort of screening before entering this type of specialty. Because the patients die and you're doing something for them every day, every day. In medical school nobody teaches us how to deal with this. It's extremely rare to find a medical school that does have some training. One I know of is Johns Hopkins. I don't know exactly how they do it. But, you know this is something that cannot be taught, but approached. And there is a way—even just the act of telling someone they have cancer, they have a terminal disease.

The patient will come to you and look to you as if you are God, and you're not. So, you can't act like that. Even though there might be some people who act like that, you know, they know everything. I'm telling you this is not true. I would not say to a patient that he or she has six months to live. I never give time. You can tell them that patients in your condition do not live long. I will tell the relatives something like that. Three months, four months, you may tell them that. You can tell someone that they look like they will die in one week, that I agree. You can take some steps toward that, but six months, I would never say that.

I use the word cancer, even though it frightens everybody, because that is what you have. You have to know what you have. The truth is also that I have been trained over the years in the revolutionary aspects of chemotherapy. Good things have come out of these treatments, even though treatments can make the patient feel worse than they are. If you know this, you know in a sense which patients you can help a little more or less. So, you have to know what the disease is and the stage, so when you are talking to the patient, you have the angel effect, you know? You can bring about a softer death, or brighter death. I do at times feel like an angel of death.

Mark: If there are no cures for a lot of these major illnesses, why do you do this? Is it to help people die?

You do, you do help people to die. It's true. You help people die. Or you think you help people to die. And I want to say that because we're doing this like this. You sit in front of somebody and start talking and say, listen you have myeloma. This disease lasts about ten to twelve years. You go through the whole thing and explain as much as you think the patient can understand. This is what we do. We really let on to as much as we think the patient wants to know honestly. A patient that is dying we don't talk too much. A patient that is asking a lot of questions we talk a little more with, and you would then talk with the relatives. I personally try to help a relative who knows everything, a relative that knows the truth, you know. And to the patient, I go along with how the patient responds. I tell the patient the truth, but sometimes I shade the truth to make the patient feel better. So whatever you can do to help you should do. But now we are talking about the physician, the comfort of that physician. Sometimes you just can't do it. You know we're not social workers, or psychologists. So, you take the medical part and you make sure it's correct. Once you make sure it's correct, you take the patient as a whole. You are a person with multiple myeloma and this is the problem. You try to prepare for yourself and the patient. I think a patient needs a safe, sound director. That's what we're here for, you know. We're not here to change anybody's mind or beliefs. I think patients need sound advice. They need to know what their alternatives are and they need to know where they can go to be able to make up their minds about things in terms of cancer. Because many times there are alternatives and they should think about them. I would never stop anybody from seeking alternative medical treatment.

I know other people that are my peers, but are not my friends, that seem to have difficulty talking about these issues. I know three or four people I can talk to, they have no problems. Let me tell you, though, the burnout rate in oncology is very high. I know oncologists who practiced for a few years and now they only do internal medicine.

The only way to dispel the myth that cancer is incurable is through some type of general education toward preventative medicine. It's the only way. Total body and mind. Total health. A way in which you brush your teeth, it's done every day. Problem is there are many other factors involved in this, like insurance companies and not enough manpower. There are advocates in the communities that do this. You know, churches, schools. It's being done, in a restricted way, it doesn't touch everybody, unfortunately.

This is a quick fix culture. Treatment in Latin countries is more comprehensive. It's a different culture, so you're not afraid of dying. Because you've been taught that if you're born, it's part of living, you're going to die. So what do you do? You make your death more bearable, if you can. And if you can't do it, it means God sent you that death. It's simple. But it's simple for me, or for somebody that believes in that. That philosophy is taught to you in your formative years. This is what is told you at school, at church, at home, in the street. This is what is taught to you. When I first came here it was culture shock. Everything. The way that people gambled with their life, and the way people don't let other people in. You put up a defense because you don't let people take advantage of you or something like that. I'm talking in general, but a lot has to do with the medical community. The first time I saw somebody in this country deal with death and dying I was taken back by the approach. It was very cold and harsh. That type of thing. Now, I think with the advent of social workers in oncology, the oncology nurses and doctors are coming together, but it goes up and down. It's still a difficult process for the patient, as well as the doctor.

You have somebody who just won't die, you understand. The ones that have so much cancer, I don't know how he's walking. Do you understand? And this is true, you see people who have a lump on their neck, you give them radiation therapy. They develop another lump on their breast, so you give them more chemotherapy. This goes on and on and on. You always have this patient, always with a complaint, always with a problem.

Mark: So the longer they live the more emotionally attached you become?

Of course, of course, this happens. And to me it's very difficult in young people. This is very difficult. I do a lot of breast cancer. And I have a lot of young women, 30–50, you know, that are active women, mothers, sisters, wives, those kind of things. And you see a little bit of their lives, you know, just slip by, you understand? You see something has changed, their sexuality changes, they don't feel as good as before, they don't care about themselves as much as before, maybe the people around them are not as warm to them. Their relationships change. And you see it, and you see it, everybody becomes like a stranger, and you become more and more, I don't know what you want to call it; the friend, the priest, the social worker, the husband, the wife. You kind of fill some sort of void for 15–20 minutes every two to three weeks or every three months. It drains you. It drains me. I see two patients like that in a week and I don't want to be on call, I just want to disappear.

We do have people that seem to just stick to you and suck a little bit out of you. Because you are the doctor, you are here to cure me, to make me feel better, you understand? And you're not doing it. But why, what is the answer? It has nothing to do with me. No, but you don't tell your patient that, but for me it is so. There is no answer to "What do I do about it?" When it happens, it happens. Yes, there are periods of very high emotional stress, extreme. And it lasts a long time, a long time. You take it with you. I have people I can talk about this with. Sometimes, you know, you talk about something like this, but it's no use talking about it, it doesn't solve the problem, you know. Doesn't solve the problem.

The problem I feel in this situation is that this is such a good person, why, why this person? It's like this happened to this person, and I'm helpless, everybody is helpless. It's like something is there that never gets answered, never gets complete. You can never put your finger on it. For example, I had this patient for five years. After a visit she comes back in eight months. I was surprised she had come back so soon for another look. We treated her with chemo, and then at the end, she just became a vegetable and lay there for three months. What happened? Nothing happened that was in my hands, it was the situation. She didn't do anything to deserve that. People just don't die, you know that. I learned very quickly in oncology they just don't die, they linger and linger and linger.

There are a lot of things that can make a patient's life easier. Pain medication will work. Don't use the term "die with dignity." There is no definition. What is dignity? You have to be alive and well to be dignified. Come on. No, I don't agree with that. I think you can die comfortably, it has nothing to do with dignity. Dignity has to do with the person, has to do with what you carry inside of you. I think everybody should have the right to die in peaceful surroundings. And I do that, okay. I have patients I can't do anything for anymore, and if there's a home to go to, I think they should go home and die. So when I talk about dignity, dignity to me is something that is in the person. That is a dignified person. In her suffering, in the last phase of her life, she may have some sort of honor or something, but the disease is not doing that to her. It comes from inside of her. But, it has nothing to do with the disease because if somebody is dying of cancer, and is having backups coming out of their breasts, there is no dignity there, you know. Not everyone can come under the category of dignity. Exactly, it's how you perceive it.

There are some people that show some kind of quality. In Spanish there is a thing that says you've got to live to know how to die. It's not what they did for 40 years it's how you did it, for yourself, nobody else, but for yourself. And I really feel that these people live that way. It's not a selfish thing. It's a conviction, a state of mind, a state of being that people have for a long time in their lives, so it went to the grave with them. I really feel that way because you see it in these people, if you're able to know a little bit about them, they have done for themselves what they wanted to do, bad, good, irrelevant. They have been able to do it. My father told me when I was ten that the world is out there for you to explore. The world is not going to come to you and if you don't take advantage of it, it will stay out there looking down on you, and you will never do anything. You have to go out there and do it and feel satisfied that you did, without harming anyone. My dad bought me my first novel. He said "Read this, and from now on read all your life." It was *War and Peace*. My father traveled all over the world and he knew what he was living for. I remember so many things that my father told me. You see you are exposed to this type of thing—cancer—and you have nothing to give. It's really sad and this is the main problem I find with people.

You have to have something to give. You have to have a story to tell. You have to have a story, a feeling. You have to have something to convey, something to radiate. If you don't have it, nobody gives it to you. You've got to reach out to people, have some kind of deep-rooted convictions. You have to be sure of certain things.

Up to now, in oncology, I'm sure I can treat the person medically. That's one thing I have to offer. I can also talk to people. I have stories, you know. I've traveled. I've met people, done things. You can give them some light into what they never had. That I did for myself. I have this idea that if I don't do things, if I don't travel, if I don't go here, if I don't talk to people I would die inside. And then what would I do, you know?

Let me tell you what is so true. You know they say the more you give the more you receive? But that's not true. You give a little here and you give a little there and something happens, you lose something. Every day you lose a little something. Yes, death gets to you. It's too close. I don't think people can accept loss so easily all the time. One time, twice, but not all the time. It's like you have no control. There comes a time when you would love to hold on to a little something. You know, just hold on to a little something that is meaningful because our death will come. I always say I'm going to open a boutique and I'm going to sell cosmetics and make-up. I always say that. I don't know why.

If you talk to people that are quote unquote dying, that have a terminal disease; you can learn so much. Let me give you an example. When I was a fellow, my boss and a nurse decided that one day we would ask every patient above the age of sixty-five, "What's the most important thing in your life?" And, "What would you have done differently if you had to live you life over again?" We found that most patients would have done things that they always wanted to do, fish, play music. People have undone things, and when you're seventy, there's no more time to do it, and now you have this terrible disease.

No, I don't fear that the longer I do this I'm losing time, losing my dreams, because I do what I want to do. I've learned to keep back a little bit for myself. Yes I do have boundaries. I think that's important. I really learned to do that. I really learned. It's very tough because people call you any time they need you and you're there. And now people know that I'm not available like that. It's been very good. This work will kind of haunt you. Even though I try and take time off for myself you remember somebody, you think about the patient, the treatment, you know. It's very depressing. No, it's not happened to me, burnout, but I'm sure that if it happened to me I would get out. I feel good, and remember I think about somebody, but it doesn't impair my functioning outside. I lead a nice life. I go out. I talk about other things. I read books. I have people I talk to about banking and other things. It's not always talking medicine and dying and death around me. It's fine. It's a good balance. And I feel refreshed after a weekend. And when I come back in, people always tell me, "Oh, it's Monday you always have to face, you know," and I say "Sure, I know what I'm going into."

* * *

Dr. Williams struck me as a warm, deep-thinking, and passionate person. We developed an immediate liking and respect for one another. Her comments on coping, communicating, and caring for terminally ill patients paint an intensely moving and rare public portrait of the frustration, anguish, and gratification of being a medical oncologist.

Dr. Williams is still an oncologist and working in the same Brooklyn office where our interview took place eight years ago. When I saw her again in early December of 1999, she was in excellent spirits and more at ease with herself and work then ever before. She is excited about the future publication of the book and wanted to know who would play her in the movie version.

DR. ADAM, ONCOLOGY FELLOW

I always say, "Nice person, bad disease," there's nothing you can do about it. The inability to help is the frustrating part of oncology. I can definitely say I get involved. More than others I get emotionally involved. What you feel when helpless is, like, you're trying to pull yourself up. The one insight is not a positive thought. You're saying, "Well, thank god it's not me. Thank god it's not my family. Thank god with the loss I'm going to go on without feeling it as much as they will." So, you have some sense of security with that. And it's not the sense of fear of death or dying that doctors feel. It's a sense of they're here, everyone goes to see an oncologist with the fear of death. Everybody. And I think what we try to do is take that fear out of the public eye by saying, "No, no the case you have may be curable." Or, "We can treat it and slow it down." So, we always offer some hope. And we hope we just hope that the statement of the hope will go from our mouths into their bodies. Not just emotionally, but physically. And that actually can help, in the sense that you gave them the best drug. You can have the best approach; they can have the best spirits, yet the disease can still overpower them. And you say, "It's not fair, it's not right." Again, the frustrating thing is there's nothing else we can do about it. Surgeons who have a patient with a disease, cut, heal, and say good-bye. And they have no emotional involvement because they never see the patient again for the most part. I think we are internists as well as oncologists, and I think we always have the sense that we'd see our patients forever and ever. And I guess when reality sets in, it's no longer forever and ever, it's a six-month encounter, and that's it. You sort of feel as if you're just seeing people at the worst times of their lives, and you just see them at their worst, which is death. And then, generally, you turn your back on them and go to your next case. You wish you could do more. What can be done about? I don't know. I mean it's just waiting for the best drug to come out, waiting for the cures of everything. Dealing with it is very frustrating, because what you want is the patient to be pain free. And a lot of patients complain, in which case, I think we just get frustrated at the patient. You know your pain is not that bad, I know you're having a little suffering if you have cancer. Trust me, everyone feels for you, but don't exaggerate, don't abuse the system. That's a fine line to delineate what a patient like that is because a patient really has pain.

I always say I'll come up with a cure, and I'll sell it to each patient one by one. I think within this field everything is working fabulously. It's a slow process. If you find a new drug it's not going to go on the market the next day. I love very much what I'm doing with medicine. I love where I am in regards to the field. I am concluding my second year as a hematology/oncology fellow. It's a field that I knew I was going to get involved with for years upon years before I even got here.

My father died when I was eleven years old, lung cancer, too young to know, too young to understand. He did not really care about taking care of himself, wanted to make sure the family had money, the family had food on the table. That was his concern. It never really became a revenge business for me. It's not as if I grew up saying, "Well, I'm going to try to cure what killed my father." My uncle, who was the head of hematology and also the assistant head of oncology at a hospital in Brooklyn, and my father's brother, became the father figure in our home. He lived maybe twenty miles away, not as if we saw him every day, or spoke with him every day, but he always oversaw that everything in the house was going well, not financially, but more emotionally. I guess my mother was filling the role of being the mother and the father of the house with three kids in the family. I'm the youngest. Some days my uncle would take me to his office. He was pretty much involved with lab research, but was, at the time, very much involved with the Israeli war and Yom Kippur war. He was head of the blood bank of Israel; they flew him out there. He has done a remarkable amount of work; in the late 60s, early 70s with cancer and hematology research. I watched him work in the lab. I didn't do work with him, I just sort of watched how he did his work and how much he loved his field. He did have patients. I saw him with his patients. He had a good rapport with them and I pretty much tried to adapt my style to the style that he had. My uncle developed Burkitt's Lymphoma, which at the time was very rare. He was married with two kids, no risk factors such as HIV. The only thing he could think of was that he contracted the disease while working in the laboratory. He had a prolonged death. Pretty much, what happened to my uncle got me into the field. He died six years after my father died. I was seventeen, eighteen at the time, and was able to understand more about the disease, saw him work, saw him with his patients, and now I saw him as a patient. The hardest thing I saw was that he was actually telling his co-workers in the lab to use him as a guinea pig to test drugs on his rare lymphoma. "Let's just try everything," he screamed and cried, but they didn't. He told to me that he wanted his work to live through me. Horrible, horrible death, it took a year and half and every day you just saw it on his face and the family. It really just hurt.

Actually I was thinking of going to dental school. Well, I loved the sciences, didn't want to bust my ass 9–5, good money. At the time my sister was living in California, married to a dentist and living comfortably. It didn't work out that way. Went to dental school at USC, but I found out that I was spending more time reading medical literature than being in the dental laboratories. So, I applied to medical school. From day one of medical school I knew I was going into hematology/oncology, no doubt. I found that my interest was pathology and really just continued on. Again, I didn't seek revenge for the deaths of my father and uncle. But I sort of wanted to continue my uncle's teaching and research and his sincerity with patients. My true test was the first day of my third year of medical school when we were thrown into the wards while doing medicine at the VA. I was given one patient that night. He was admitted the night before and had colon cancer, late stage. Chemotherapy was not going to do anything for him. Basically, what he needed was supportive care, pain management. A nurse called me around 10 P.M., saying "the patient's in pain do you just want to give him morphine now, a little push, and then we just give him a push every hour. Or, do you just want to give him one push, and cover him for two or three hours, and we'll just be through with it." So I said, "No, no let's give it to him." I also said I would like to speak with him. I spoke with him and he said he was in pain now and what usually helps him is when he gets the pain medication every hour. So I asked my resident and he said, "Yeah give it to him every hour, but you have to be at the bedside, you have to push the morphine, nurses don't do it." So I sat and talked with him all night. Didn't go to sleep. We talked about his understanding of his disease. How he feels about it, what he can do about the cancer. He understood the fact that he was going to die and that the most important thing he said he was doing over the last few months was taking care of business. He made sure that his family was taken care of in regards to financial security, education, and future. He had come to terms with his family, his disease and really was, at this time, feeling satisfied with where he was, and the understanding that he was going to die and accepted it.

I was going through memories, more of my uncle than my father. My father was more of a shock to me than anything else was. We were in summer camp when he went for his operation. They found out that he pretty much metastasized everywhere by the time he sought out medical attention. They took him to a Houston hospital for experimental therapy. We didn't know that this was usually done, and we didn't know about chemotherapy. It was kept away from the kids. With my uncle we saw it. We understood it. Of course I understood his business, so I knew what he was going through. So when I was helping this gentlemen in the hospital I was just reflecting upon my uncle being sick. I took a wink somewhere around five or six and when I woke up this patient had passed away. My reaction was surprise. Surprise that it had been so fast, that it wasn't a whole commotion of his heart stopping, having pain or him saying, "I can't believe." He just went quietly. His wife was there for most of the evening. When she came back the resident said to me "Tell the wife." And then the intern came and said, "No, no, I'll tell the wife," which I felt much better about because you don't want to get thrown in to the profession too fast. I went home that day stunned. You know I've seen my uncle, after he passed away, but I never saw a patient dead right in front of me. I was pretty concerned with how I would deal with it. With this person passing away, I sort of understood that the best way to deal with it was to talk about it. I came home and told my mother the story, you know telling my mother the story in which her husband and brother-in-law died of cancer is not the best thing in the world. And telling her I'm going into oncology, well, it just brings back horrible memories for her. Her dealing with it has definitely improved over the years, but at this time it wasn't good, and I just couldn't find enough people to talk to about it. I found a friend I went to college in New York with. We talked about. He was more in the sense of "Let's go out to dinner." And I just got it off my chest. I don't know what he heard or what he cared to hear, but we never discussed it again. I think it just went in one ear and out the other.

Why does our culture deny death so much? Well, I think people accept the fact that people die after a heart attack much quicker than people dying of cancer. Would one rather have a person like my uncle, who for a year and a half suffered and then deal with the suffering over a year and half, and feel a little relieved that finally the suffering has ended. Or, to deal with a person that we knew in our family, a health nut, ran, jogged, played tennis, did everything, cholesterol was like beautiful, and doctors were treating him as a prize patient. He was in his sixties, played tennis at a hotel over a holiday and dropped dead. Family couldn't deal with it. No one could deal with it, and after the shock hit. So what would you want? Would you want someone who passes away very fast, who you never had a chance to say good-bye to, or would you want someone who's been suffering? You know I don't think there's a good answer for that either.

Mark: Well, you just mentioned a scenario with a heart attack and everything you mentioned was a condition of my father when he dropped dead on a tennis court from a heart attack.

Dr. Adam: Really? I'm sorry to hear that.

Mark: No, that's ok. So, I hear what you are saying and I empathize, obviously, with what you are saying as well. But, I think were talking about the same thing.

Dr. Adam: Right, ok.

Mark: Openness.

Dr. Adam: Death.

Mark: We see that a lot of people don't communicate. Whether it's from a heart attack, or cancer, AIDS or any life-challenging illness, there is denial.

There doesn't have to be denial, because no one, everyone wants to think either that one, they're immortal, or two they think of today, don't think about tomorrow. Enjoy today. You have to really live for what you can live for now and you can't think of the future, when it comes to dying, death I mean. I thought about this today. Today is a Jewish holiday, so there is a memorial service. I was at services and the Rabbi said, "Reflect upon the person who passed away." The first thing that came to my mind was that I was calculating my father's age. He passed away twenty years ago, and I was saying he would be sixty-nine. That means at this time of my life I would have been preparing for his eminent death. I said this probably when I was fifteen, sixteen years old. And I know it's a stupid statement to say, and it's very selfish, but, I said I would rather have been young and not know and dealt with my father's death then, then suffer with it after I've built up a relationship with him over the years. Eleven years old, eleven and half years old with a person you see for a day and a half, two days if you include Friday afternoons, weeknights, every other night maybe. I seem to remember my spankings very well, but I'm saying it hurt, it hurt badly. You just walk around saying, I mean, at eleven years old everyone says to you, "Oh, what's with your parent's house? And like the word is, you know, I don't have parents. I have a parent. You go to camp you're meeting someone and everything just stirs back your father's memory.

I would inform a child in what the child can understand about the disease process. I can't anticipate or expect them to grieve in the sense that we would grieve because they haven't seen grief. They can understand that it's sad. They can understand that they'll never see the person again, that time moves on, and one can just live with happy memories. Again, it was easier for me to have dealt with it back then and not have to deal with it now. My mother had remarried and I love my stepfather. He is sixty-five years old and eventually he'll move on too and hopefully will not pass away for many, many, many more years to come. Dealing with that will be much easier than dealing with my real father passing away.

Going back to the whole communication aspect. The girl I was dating when I was in college passed way from leukemia. She was twenty-five. What happened was all our friends went to visit her and heard she had AML. From what I understood of AML her survival was not good. She looked great, conversed fine. We laughed and no one brought up the disease, no one asked her what happened or anything like that. Uh, because I don't think you go to a hospital to visit a patient about their disease, unless if you are older. I think older patients can talk about their disease to friends. Younger patients do not because I think they are embarrassed about their disease and they don't want their friends to know what might happen to them. I think they should talk with their family, to their best friend. I think it's probably best to keep it from other friends unless you feel strongly about talking to them about it. Let's go back to my girlfriend's visit. We left the hospital in the afternoon. We stayed together from about three through nine o'clock. We ended up going to dinner and a movie. During this time all I would talk about was I can't believe she is going to die, I can't believe she is going to die. The whole time everyone says to be quiet. And I realized that I had to get it off my chest and I talked about it. I didn't eat dinner. I didn't enjoy the movie. When I came home I felt ok. I felt I got it off my chest. She died five months later. I got a call from Carol, one of the friends who I went to visit in the hospital with and she was devastated. "God, she was so young." And I said I understand. She said you don't sound shocked, you don't sound sad." She was crying. I told her I dealt with it back when I visited her and I'm very sad, and its shocking news, but I'm not devastated.

It is a mortality thing. Right, she was very close to my age. What makes me think I'm not going to be dead soon. And that's when I realized, that is exactly when I realized that you have to really communicate, talk to people about it. I mean I come home to a wife who hates hearing about it but she definitely listens to everything I say. She sees me sad and she gives me all the medals of honor for dealing with it, how could you, and god I'm proud of you and your very special, you're the kind of person who can deal with it. I don't come home as much as I used to and say "God I saw a case that I feel horrendous about." It's now once in a while. I think that now I don't have to talk about it to get it off my chest. I deal with it by talking to the patient about it. I follow my uncle's philosophy, be honest, tell them what they have and how involved it is, and what can be done, if anything can be done. Always offer them treatment options if one is available. Talk to the patients about everything. I saw a gentleman a couple a days ago, but first I'll give you the more general routine. You come to the patient, "How are you. My name is doctor so and so." I don't tell them my profession here, they would not know what an oncologist means, anyway. You have to tell them you're a cancer doctor. Ask them how they are feeling. Welcome them to the hospital. I don't really hit them with the whole history because I've already read the chart. I know if I have a physical finding, I know what I want to look for, I know what they found before in the past on this chart. So I know really how to direct this exam. I know how to direct my question. I don't feel it is my job to belabor past information that was obtained. He doesn't have to tell me his whole medical histories, allergies, I know that. I know I just want to talk to the patient. I don't want him to feel like he is giving me his life story. I want to find out what his complaint is, find out how he has been, what they've done for it in the hospital, what tests they've done for him in the hospital, what he may understand the disease to be and what have they (attendees) told him. And with that knowledge we talk.

This gentleman I saw a couple of days ago is pretty bad off. Has lost a lot of weight, just does not feel good, doesn't look good, but is a knowledgeable individual. I introduce myself, my name is so and so, how are you feeling, that whole spiel. "What have they told you?" I ask him. "About what," he responds. "Well have they done any tests while you were in the hospital?" "Yes they put a needle into my liver." "Have they explained to you what the results showed?" I asked. "I don't remember," he said. "Did they do any other tests?" He says "Well, yes, they gave me an X-ray on the _____" which is a bone scan and "what did that show?" "They didn't tell me."

So I found out that the biopsy came back positive for cancer cells. He says, "That's right, I remember that, yes." I feel a little better that he knew that, that it didn't come from me, but at the same time it still feels like shit that you have to tell a person this is the disease. So I remind myself that I am an oncologist, I am a cancer doctor. Throughout this whole time you have to see what kind of patient you are dealing with when you first start talking with them. In some hospitals they are more understanding, knowledgeable and they want to be helped. In other hospitals you may just, it depends on the person, may just be another piece of meat. Or you may be a nice guy. My uncle never did this, but if I have the opportunity I sit on their bed. May hold their hand, depending on the person. It's really something you have to just sense, really, you can't go in saying my approach is going to be this. You have to see how they talk to you. You have to see a look in their eye of like, I can trust you or I need to be held, or something. No, I didn't hold this gentleman's hand. I had, he was lying down, and I had my hand on his knee. You know there was always contact between us, there were times during the talking that he took his arm and placed it on my arm. I explained to him his disease. In this case he had adenocarcinoma, spread to the liver, probably the spleen, lymph nodes in that area, but they did not know where his primary disease was. His bone scan basically lit up every bone in his body. We talked for forty-five minutes about adenocarcinoma with an unknown primary and what it actually means. He was pretty much in bed the whole time. I discussed with him his options, if we find a primary diagnosis for the disease, or we don't find a primary diagnosis. I explained to him in his case there is a good chance that the prostate is a primary, there is a chance that with chemotherapy you could have a response. However, if it's not from the prostate, pretty much the survival is limited. He didn't ask me how long that was. And I debated whether to tell him what the survival for this type of cancer is. If they ask me I tell them in concrete terms how much longer they have to live. I quote them, well let me tell you what I told him in this case. I told him if was prostate the numbers are different and you could put yourself in that category because you have some liver disease also and that it does respond with the chemotherapy. He said to me that you are the first person to tell me that at least there is some glimmer of hope. I said that you have to understand something, the chance that it is from prostate is small, but, here is that glimmer of hope and that's what you should hold onto. He asked me, "Is there a chance that I could be cured?" I said we would not know that until one, we know it is from the prostate, and two we see your response from the chemotherapy. After we have better insight into how you respond we can talk about it. I told him that if it is anywhere else but the prostate I'm not offering any treatment because one, it can do more harm than good and two, my approach is not to just increase your survival but to increase your quality of life. And if you are going to live four months I want you to live four months with no knowledge of pain. Enjoy the family, they can spend time with you, you don't have to be in a hospital. He understood. He appreciated it. I asked if he had any family members, if he wants to go home, to whom to go to. He has a sister in the St. Lawrence River area; it is beautiful there. I recently found out the she is really to old to tend for him, so we discussed options of where to go, nursing homes, hospices. He said to me, "If you tell me I should give up then I'll give up. You gave a glimmer of hope, I'm looking for that glimmer of hope right now." You feel good when you hear it. And you just walk out of the room, trying to paint a realistic picture. I didn't try to paint a picture of glory that he didn't deserve, but you always walk out of the room saying "Nice guy, bad disease." I went to the phone, called the urologist and told him I wanted him to see him right away. So I mean, you try.

I individualize patients, different kinds of diseases. If you feel that a patient can undergo chemotherapy, tolerate it, I always offer it, regardless if there is a glimmer of hope or no cure whatsoever, because 10 percent of the patients live. How do I know this is not the one out of ten that is going to live? Depends on the patient at the time. If I see an 80-year-old person, who doesn't walk around, confined to a bed, lives alone, and is miserable, I'm not going to offer him anything. I see a 45-year-old guy with a family, whose family depends upon him, who needs that glimmer of hope, I'm going to offer him everything, first line, second line, surgery, radiation. I would offer him everything I could. See a woman at sixty, children are out of the house, she's diagnosed with cancer I always approach it if this was a family member of mine would I offer them chemotherapy? Would I want her to endure it? I probably would, in this case, offer two cycles. I say, "Promise me two cycles." We'll do the CAT-scan again to see if you tumor goes away. If the tumor grows, I'm going to stop it right there. I may change the drug; I'll see how you tolerate the chemotherapy. If the tumor shrinks obviously you're going to continue it. If doesn't change I'd like to give you another cycle on it and see how you do.

> Mark: Is it this glimmer of hope for a cure that gets you up everyday? Is that what it is?

It's more when you improve the quality of life. You're doing that in a way that takes their pain away. You take away the pain of the disease emotionally, they now don't have cancer any more or their cancer's getting smaller. When you give them that knowledge, there's definitely that aspect of more hope among the patients, which gives them a stronger emotional approach to the disease. They may find things are a little doubtful, but if they feel their cancer's getting smaller, that's great news. Now they feel I have to fight a little more, and it goes away a little more. So, when you give them the clinical response positive, you're giving them both a physical and emotional response positive. That glimmer of hope that you give them helps the patient understand that yes it's going to be an uphill battle, and yes, I think we can overcome this disease if we deftly approach it with this type of medication or this approach of therapy. I tell my patients when I feel that they're gonna give up hope, or if they're gonna start therapy and they approach it more like, I don't care approach, I say, "It has to come from here" and I point to the heart. I say "If you don't have this, I don't care what you have up in your head, it's really in the heart. You can say to yourself "I'm feeling pain" but if you feel stronger off it, you can overcome this, and you can beat it, that's your first step. I mean, they always say that alcoholics, the first sign of treatment is by acknowledging the fact that you're an alcoholic. I said you have to understand that you have to deal with it, and you have to fight it, not only for yourself, but for your family. You need them, they need you. I don't paint a picture, actually I can't say that. If I find an anxious patient who needs to hear what they have to hear and disease is everywhere, I may paint them a picture that there's a chance, 20 percent, but it's a chance, that they're gonna have a response. If I see the response after two months worsening than I may paint them a bad picture. If I see that it's gotten better, I then feel very good about them and to myself that we're at least approaching it, and trying to at least get a good response. I think once you offer something to a patient, you have to follow through with it. When we say the word "we can give you" that's what they hold onto, they hold onto the hope that "yeah, well, I have options and I can do something with it." I always anticipate that I'm gonna be the person who's willing to cure everybody. That I have this approach of we can deal with it, you'll get rid of it, then you'll be better. I'll save everybody. No, it's not happening.

I can safely say no one has fallen through the cracks that did not get offered what he or she should have gotten. I don't know if you have heard of the Friday Conferences, where we are told to give patients this drug, try them on protocol. And for the most part that stays in that room. I mean they want me to put patients on protocol, and I find that I have a drug that works just as fine. What it does is to get patients enrolled onto a study and prove numbers are good or bad.

Putting patients on a study is the goal for this hospital, because you get grant money. Priorities are priorities. This is not my concern, here. My concern is more to give them what I think can work, and give them a shot. My patients don't have to be guinea pigs. My patients don't have to sit through biopsies, suffer through investigational drugs, and feel like they're a guinea pig. If I tell them I have an investigational drug they think everything else is finished. If patients have become refractive to chemotherapy, and I see an end to it, and that they are not going to respond well, I will then offer them a drug instead of chemotherapy—an experimental drug.

Is there a cure? Honestly, with cancer, for the most part, you're not going to cure them. Your are prolonging their life, which in some instances is prolonging the agony, pain, and the suffering of not only them, but of their family around them. Now you tie in the whole aspect of shock of the disease. Umm, not really depression yet, and it's not really denial. That's why I really feel that you have to talk with them about the disease, to strengthen them if they ask for definite survival numbers and if those numbers can be improved with chemotherapy or surgery, or radiation. Right there you bypass denial, they're hearing the numbers associated with what they have, they're hearing options. So it's no longer denial. I mean it's very hard to accept right off the bat, but reality is painting a picture in that they can understand what they have. The patients don't want to die. They want to live forever. They will do what it takes to live forever. If it requires undergoing surgery or chemotherapy they will do it because they want to live. But they want to live, I think for the most part, for other people, family, spouses for the most part.

You see if the patient is stable enough to deal with the disease. You see if the patient would benefit from chemotherapy. Are you improving someone's quality of life? You have to again, individualize it, and see what the person wants out of life. Do they want to undergo therapy? Are they stable enough emotionally to deal with the side effects of chemotherapy? Do they have a strong support group around them to push them forward, and say listen, "We can be there for you. We're always there for you."

I think working with this approach you can hold onto life more than holding on or preparing for death. And when you quote numbers, you don't quote numbers saying 70 percent of the people die, you quote 30 percent of the people live. And that's what they want to hear. The numbers may not be good, but they don't want to hear the word death. And my patient who I told a few days ago that if the cancer's not in his prostate, he does not have long to live, I said I cannot anticipate your life being that much longer. I did not say I think you will die. They can be scared of the word death or die. At the time he was very realistic with the fact that his disease went to the liver, which means death. I never said the word death. I approach it in a different light.

It can never be taught. I had the early education of my uncle, and what he did. How much of it stuck, how much of I am I making up, how much of it am I applying, I can't even think. If you think about it, doctors love to stand around a patient who's lying down, cause it gives them a sense of authority. I throw that away when I sit on a patient's bed. Right, I break that wall. I'm a friend, I'm a human being, I can look you straight in the eye, I'm not looking down upon you, I can hold your hand, I'm not distant from you. I'm there. And I find it easier to have contact for me to talk to them, than for me not to, rather than have my hands in my pocket and look down upon them saying, "Oh yes, you have cancer." Then it's a cold hearted individual, a hot shot doctor saying to me that he knows something I don't know, and that's simply where it ends. Listen to patients, rather than you tell them your standard lines. They appreciate it and they feel that they can trust you, and I think once the trust is there, the communication is always improved.

In my medical school, first year you have medical ethics, but they don't talk about this. Ironically, they had a *JAMA* article titled "It's Over Debbie." This came out in 1985 or '86, and it was written by a gynecology resident. No one knows if it was real or fictitious. It was about a person who came to the bedside of a young girl, with the mother by the bedside. The patient had ovarian cancer, a lot of pain, and he describes how to calculate the morphine dose to help with pain control. And then he added on like double that, so he wanted just to kill her. And her mother said, "Help her get rid of her pain forever." The doctor said to the patient, "Is this what you want me to do? Patient said, "Yes." Gave it, and the last line was, "It's over Debbie." And no one knows if it's a real article, or if someone wrote it and should go after this guy, or if it was just to stir conversation. Do doctors talk about it? No. We don't talk about it. Kervorkian's doing things, we all pat Kervorkian on the back. Can we do what he is doing in public? No. Can't do it.

Yes, there is a certain place for letting go. But, again is it ego, or is it the patient's quality of life? Does the doctor want to push the patient by giving him more treatment and have the patient sort of emotionally and physically divorced? Or, do you want to have the patient be comfortable and let the patient have some dignity, and if they're going to die let them die like a man, not die like a dog. Doctors sense they have to do everything in their power. And if one chemotherapy doesn't work, give another, that doesn't work I have a third one, or I have an experiment or I can throw you to Sloan-Kettering, they have drugs that we haven't been able to hear about.

Doctors sort of tell you this is what you have, this is what we're going to do about it, and this is what I would recommend. Sometimes they don't even say, "What do you think," or "How would you like to approach it." If there is an option of no treatment versus treatment that is probably the only time a patient has a say in the matter. Most times, when patients come to doctors as referral or an outpatient, they're asking for treatment, so it seems as if they're willing to undergo anything the doctor recommends. We've definitely seen physicians who are very compassionate with their patients, and don't offer them anything. It depends on the physician. You're dependent on the physician. Some physicians over-treat, I don't think its' more for the fact that want to offer patients a better chance. I think they would like to see what happens. If it turns out to be great, then they'll continue chemotherapy. If the patient has a demise because of the over-treatment, then, you know, they gave it a shot.

Who is to say whether it's rationale or they really want to build up their bill? We have our conferences and we hear their (attendees') thoughts. Some doctors give drugs that have not been proven to show any benefit, but they still push it because they say it's a better agent. Why? Their experience. Why do some doctors offer chemotherapy to patients who don't need it? Maybe they feel if the patient can benefit from it, it gives them a sense of security, in that he has a patient who feels if he dies, fine, compared to the patient dying without trying.

I tend to go with standard care. I tend to do what I think is best for the patient, knowing that the patients have all their trust in me, it's your decision. There's really a fine line when to treat and when not to. When a patient says yes and you say no, and when you say yes and the patient says no. Obviously, when the patient says no it ends right there.

If you say no and the patient says yes, what would I tend to do? Even if I paint them a bad picture, and they say, "I want it." Even if I tell them the survivals going to be nothing, that you're going to die like a dog, and it's very disgusting, and their very insistent, I have to offer them therapy. I give them the little small print, saying, "I'm going to give two cycles. We'll repeat the test, the blood test, repeat the CAT-scans and if I see no change, I am definitely going to stop it, and that's that. I don't feel it's worthwhile."

You just try and do what you can do, and if it's not physically with the medication, it has to be emotionally. You have to give them your all. I mean, three o'clock in the morning phone calls you don't usually get, but if it's in the office, close the door, and offer to spend a little more time. It's hard in the real world. When push comes to shove what do you do? Say, I'll have the patient come back and I'll spend, as my last appointment, time with them and talk with them and let them express themselves, or go home that night and say, "So long, I'll call you later?"

I'd rather throw some things away for tomorrow and spend time with a new patient. I definitely see it as being efficient with your time. Some people I see leaving at 5 P.M., they have to go home. Some people stay later. I mean, again, it's your approach to the patient. Your introduction to a new patient is going to definitely leave an impact on them, forever. If you sit and explain to them everything, you answer their questions, you give them all the time in the world they will think the world of you. When you're doing your residency, patients want to know a lot of information. You can either blow them off and say, "Well, you know this is just the way it is and don't worry about, it'll go away," or "You have this and you'll deal with it." Or you can sit and talk with them and explain the disease process, what they can do to prevent, what they can do to heal and how to approach it the next time it happens. Internships are always a bad year. You have no time for helping. Residency, second year, is a lot easier. Third year, again, if you're efficient with your time, you can do it.

I can see among the fellows, some people just want to do their job and move on. Some people want to get, I can't say emotionally involved, but supportive of the patient, and let the patient know what to expect, what is happening right now, and what can be happening in the future. I think if you deal with it right here and now, an educated patient is always a better patient. If the patient comes to you and says, "Hi doc, treat me, good-bye," you think maybe they are just going through the motions to live, or do they actually have a reason to really enjoy life?

No, no, most doctors do not offer time or communicate effectively on these issues. It's easier not too. It may be their own denial construct, it may also be the fact that why should they talk at length with the patient about it if it doesn't have to be dealt with right now. It may be they have no time in their office to see a patient, talk to them openly and discuss future thoughts about death. A lot of doctors don't want patients to hear the word because now they're going to think they don't believe in the doctor. I don't think they behave this way because it's a fear of their own mortality. When I talk about death with patients I'm a little anxious. It's very uncomfortable. I definitely feel, as we say, pitted out. You'd say I was a little sweaty over there. I've found that you have to just sort of talk clearly, look them in the eye and hold their hand and talk. Why don't doctor's do that? I can't answer why they can't do it. Maybe it's fear that their own personal statistics are going to go down, that they actually are not helping patients in their own field, or why can't their patient live longer than other patients can. I don't feel that, guilt, so I don't know if others can. I don't go to sleep waking up in a cold sweat. I sleep well because everything is off my chest. Everything is out in the open.

I personally do not fear my own death. I think I accept it. Only you see, no one can ever accept one's own death. I can talk about it because I've seen death close. With my father I obviously didn't express it because I didn't know. My uncle, I was too young really to learn how to express it. But it was with that patient, my first patient. I didn't know this person. I ended up being in a seven and half hour conversation with a stranger, who moved me, made me feel about the past, made me try to offer him hope. And at the same time I know I'm helping him because my job there was giving him morphine every hour. And it's what he wanted it's what I knew I was helping with. And, I think he sensed that the fact that I would rather give him the drug every hour the way he wanted it, the way he'd be more comfortable, than just sort of give morphine, run away for two or three hours, then come back and say, "You need more"? I mean that's obviously the first time I sat and talked with a patient. This whole thing is about finding life meaningful in death. There's that famous line "The goal of our practice is really not to add years to life, but life to years."

Would it help if doctors talked about these issues? I don't know. It's very personal. I mean, I think of fellows that I work with, I think maybe one or two people can talk about it. Others become very short in the conversation, or they have become cynical over the years and don't feel talking to the patient about death is a conversation, it's more like you're telling them they're going to die. And they may fear the patient will now walk around saying we talked about death in my doctor's office. Another reason doctors can't get together and talk about these things is time. You work from eight, eight-thirty until five, study from seven to eight the last thing you want to do when you finish your day is talk shop. You want to go home, be with family, and relax. A lot of people don't need to talk about it. A lot of people simply put themselves in front of the television, listen to music, go for a walk and get it out of their system. Whether they deal with it or they just block it, it is their own way of dealing with it. I definitely know that the attendees we work with enjoy life. I know some of their out-of-hospital hobbies and they live life to the fullest. They definitely have their interests.

Yes, the support system outside of the hospital is extremely important. It definitely is the life force. It's a good point. As much as life dies in front of you, you can develop life in a compensating space. Well, being recently married, my wife expectant, I think the most important thing to me, as I go through all this, is my family. I mean, you have to live everyday for what it offers. I come home, deal with my work, put that aside, spend as much time with my wife as possible, and rub her belly to make sure the baby knows that I'm there. With my father not being home when I was younger overcompensates me wanting to be there for the family. I'm very much interested in sports, travel, and theater. We met here, while I worked in hematology. She has been with me through this tough stretch of oncology. It was a quick engagement, quick marriage. Eight months from start to finish, and then we were married for two months, and now she's pregnant. It sounds sick, but I know her like a book, and I'm getting to know her more. My time is with her. It's exactly where I want to be. My interests only lie with my wife and my future child. We still do what we want to do, but I'm happy as a clam just to sit there knowing that's she's either in the other room or next to me. No, absolutely not. She's not a physician. I could never date a physician. I could never take the shit that I give out. I just don't want to come home and talk shop. I'd like to have my world more diverse. I don't want to hear myself every night.

Sometime I fantasize about being Michael Jordan. He offers something I can never offer and what I can offer something he can never offer. I can never entertain the world like he does. I can never make the 35.9 million dollars he does. He has financial security, but I have an emotional sense of security. I know I can help people right now. And I know I can always help people. I know in the long term, he's going to be who he is, he's going to be famous. He enlightens children; he gives them a shining light. Someone has to be, most of us, on the bottom doing the dirty work, and I guess that's what I am. I would love to make thirty-five million dollars a year. I'd love to make one million dollars a year in this field, be more comfortable and not have to work as much as I do. I'm very happy where I am. Again, this is something that through my teenage years I saw myself doing. I'm living out what I wanted to be. I feel very comfortable about it.

*　　*　　*

Dr. Adam was an exceptionally expressive and patient-centered physician. He provides new and seasoned healthcare providers with a broad look inside the reasons why someone may become an oncologist, sensitive ways in which to interact with patients, and cope in and out of work.

I spent more time interviewing Dr. Adam than any other individual. I felt I related to him more than others because of how the death of his dad and uncle inspired him to pursue a career in medicine. Since his fellowship, Dr. Adam has been working as an oncologist in both private practice and hospitals outside the New York metropolitan area.

DR. RICHARDS, ONCOLOGY FELLOW

I accept death with clarity, knowing its just part of the life process. You only get one life. You only go around once so you might as well enjoy what time you have. You got a life and you live it. You enjoy yourself and do whatever you want to do to the fullest.

I'm currently an oncology fellow. This is my third year and I'm doing a year of research, spending most of my time in the laboratory, but

I still go to the clinic once a week. I have about 45 to 50 patients I follow. My first year here I was doing hematology. As a resident I was interested in hematology and rheumatology, among other things, and initially looked around for rheumatology fellowships. When I interviewed for these positions I began to realize that most of what rheumatology is taking care of patients with arthritis, more than anything else. The type of rheumatology patients that most interested me were vasculitis patients, which are somewhat sicker, or almost like dead. A lot of rheumatologists don't even particularly want to see too many such patients.

So then I thought about hematology, a subject I always liked when I was a medical student and then as a resident, when I saw lots of great hematology cases. Lots of leukemia, lymphoma, which I always thought, was kind of neat. What kept me from wanting to do hematology, even when I finally decided to try it but was still a little bit resistant to the idea, was the fear, if you will, of oncology. That's partially based on what I saw as a resident. The institution at which I served my residency is interesting because the medicine service is a division of neoplastics, which is separate from the department of medicine. They have their own floor, and the fellows are sort of the house staff and you don't have very many interactions with those patients who are on protocol and with those patients who are more interesting. You tend to see patients who are being followed by private doctors in the community who have many privileges at this institution. The patients are either so sick that they need to be in the hospital because they're failing, or they're at a point where they're sick enough that they can't get chemotherapy as an outpatient. So that's your only real interaction with the oncology patient, and you get a very skewed view of what oncology is. That's why at that time oncology was not particularly interesting to me. All you have are broken down patients at the end stage of their game, basically. I hadn't seen the other parts of the patient, the fact that they were being followed for months and months beforehand. It's a shock. In hematology you get a good sense of what being a hematologist is. You see inpatients constantly. You do bone marrows. But the house staff does not see oncology patients in general unless you end up on the medicine service, by which time the patient is generally sick. You don't see the very sick patients most of the time because the sick oncology patient is really sick. It's actually post-op diagnoses and these are a much different group of patients, much healthier groups of patients with whom you have a lot more interactions. You can do a lot more. Help a lot more. Occasionally you get patients on medicine services that have been diagnosed with lung cancer who are still pretty healthy, but oftentimes you don't see that. You don't usually get to see the breast cancer patient who's getting chemotherapy. They're not on the medicine service and you don't necessarily know what goes on in the oncology outpatient center. So for the most part, the rheumatologist doesn't see terminal end-stage patients. Certainly not as much as in oncology.

Leukemics are in general oftentimes exciting patients, and more times than not, they are terminal patients. You can do a lot for them. The patho-physiology is very neat and interesting. In a patient who's known to have lung cancer it's different. That's work, a lot more work. The other thing is work, too, but it's work where the patient is really sick and we're going to do something for him. You're going to do a lot for this leukemia patient. He's going to get chemotherapy; his white count's going to come down. You haven't really attempted to cure this patient. I don't think the attitude is there to cure this one cancer patient. When we get in control of the patient the attitude is that the patient has a curable disease. So a lot of times terminal patients are diagnosed as "curable." More so on the hematology side than on the oncology side. There's more hope in hematology. Chances are there's nothing you can do for a patient with acute lung cancer. He'll be dead in a month; probably less.

I finally decided to go for it in hematology/oncology because they're sort of combined. I talked to some oncologists and, strangely enough, some of them had had similar thoughts or fears, if you want to use that word. They knew they liked hematology but they weren't at all sure about oncology; they thought they would dislike it. And these are people who are doing 90 to 95 percent of their work in oncology. A lot of them found they really enjoyed it, so I decided to go that route. I was very pleasantly surprised at how much I've enjoyed oncology.

It's very different following these patients as outpatients; when they're healthier we can still do a lot of good for them. You try to prevent their getting into trouble from metastatic disease later on. These are patients with whom you didn't really have much contact with before, but now are relatively healthy, so it helps your mindset. You're going to move away from anybody who's going to "die." A lot of these people will do fairly well.

Another thing I like about oncology is you end up dealing with lots of different people and services; you're dealing with radiologists and pathologists looking at slides. All this type of stuff is neat. It's fun. Taking care of patients is sometimes problematic.

With some patients there's a language problem which makes it difficult to fully explain their situation. There's also somewhat of a lack of sophistication so that you sometimes wonder if they have a good feel of what's really going on. You wonder what their concept is of their disease and if they understand their prognosis. It's hard to say if the information is not being understood or if the patient just doesn't want to hear. If the patient speaks English well and is intelligent, you have a better idea of what's denial and what's not being understood.

I have a 40-year-old patient, a real nice lady, who has a tumor. It hasn't gotten any smaller, but it hasn't grown. It's sort of stable. I've been explaining to her that this is a good thing but she keeps trying to find out how much more chemotherapy she needs and when we're going to stop it. She asks, "Why isn't the tumor going away?" I'm like, "Yeah, the tumor's not going away, but it's not growing. And we're perfectly happy doing this." I've explained to her a lot that she's likely to die from this disease, but two years from now, not two knots from now, as long as she's tolerating the chemotherapy reasonably well. This woman isn't like someone who has cancer. She dresses sharply. She's healthy looking. She's tolerating it fine. It's not even as though it's hurting her quality of life significantly. So it's a little upsetting to me sometimes because I spend all this time explaining the situation to her and on her next visit she'll ask exactly the same questions and we'll have exactly the same discussion. She doesn't speak English perfectly well. She was born in China but I think she has a grasp of this thing. The bottom line is you're still telling them bad news and they're looking for good news. It's as though they think if they keep asking the same questions, maybe they'll get the answers they want, which is that we're stopping the therapy tomorrow. "It's all gone away and you don't need any more treatment." This hasn't happened, though, and it's not going to happen.

You always have denial. Bad things can happen to others but they're not going to happen to you. Denial is an amazing thing. It was frightening in a way when one of my medical school roommates was diagnosed with metastatic sarcoma just as he was finishing his residency. By this time we had drifted apart over a period of three years and the only reason I would be talking to him would be because he is sick and my field is hematology and oncology. But is this what this person needs to hear, to talk about? The worst part is that this guy was going to be doing a urology fellowship starting next year. So it's like, what am I going to talk to him about? Should I talk to him about what I'm learning in oncology and hematology when here he is, sitting with his metastatic sarcoma which is eventually going to kill him? This is what went on in my head. Maybe it would have been a little different if we hadn't drifted apart, if it was someone I'd stayed closer to.

In oncology, in particular, there are no cures, but that's also true in other parts of medicine. In just about all the fields of internal medicine there are patients who are going to die. I think dealing with HIV patients is even worse than what I do. In oncology, most of the patients you're going to see are 60, 70, or 80 years old. You don't see too many 20- or

30-year-olds, thank God, because that would be much harder to deal with. I had a group of HIV patients in my clinic, 25 years old, 28, and 36. It's really heartbreaking. These are people who have never had a chance to accomplish what they had the potential to accomplish. They're just getting started. With someone who's 65 or 70 it's sad, but they've at least reached a point where they've raised their families and have accomplished a lot. It's sort of the winding down of your life, if you will, rather than getting to the point where you're life is just staring to get going. It's tough.

Sometimes you have patients you can talk to and sometimes you have a little bit more time to talk to a person and ask how they're doing. Occasionally there have been times when I've done this. I had a patient; a 40-year-old married woman with cervical cancer. She was incredibly bright. She was with it. She had had all kinds of hardships in the past and had gotten her act together. And then she was diagnosed with cervical cancer in an advanced stage. She got radiation therapy and chemotherapy and did well for about six months or so. Over a span of two or three months she suddenly crashed. Quickly. She dealt with things so well. I'm sure she was in pain. It was an ugly situation and I felt bad for her husband. His mother and sister had both recently died of cancer in the last year and a half, and here he was watching his wife in her pain and suffering. They were obviously close. They were nice people. Good, solid people. I really felt bad for him. I tried talking to him and being a little bit supportive, even though a lot of it is lip service in a way because the person realizes it's just the thought that you care enough to ask. But what are you saying? There's really nothing you can say, but you care enough to ask. I really felt bad for this woman. I liked her and it was painful to watch her in total agony when she was dying, becoming less and less of a person and more and more of a cancer patient. The stick figure, if you will, a pain-racked person who couldn't do anything. It was painful. There wasn't anything I could do for her. People die. You didn't give them their disease.

The real thing at issue is that when you first get the patient with cancer, you know she's going to die. You know the kind of cancer she has. You know the therapy is out there but you know she's going to have to die. The challenge is to try to establish a relationship with this person. Get to like this person. That's the challenge. The easy way is to stay distant all the time and say to yourself, fine, this person's going to be dead in a year and a half, two years, and I'm not going to get close to the patient. I know this is going to happen so why should I bother letting myself care about somebody, be concerned about somebody, who I know is going to die? That's the easy situation. That's the easy way to do it: do nothing.

I've been told there are times, when the patient is dying, that the physician runs away. The last three to four weeks of a patient's terminal illness they leave all sorts of responsibilities to the family, the nurses, and the social workers, for emotional support. On the other hand, I also sometimes find out that there are some doctors who can't let go and they'll jack up the treatment. There are oncologists who will give everybody a type of chemotherapy initially and then see what happens. See how the patient responds. I know other people who do nothing. Just wait and see what happens. Maybe do something later. Who's right? They're both right.

It's important to get close to the patient and the family, but not too close. In the back of your mind you always have to keep the reality that this patient is going to die. As an oncologist you probably won't let yourself get too close with most or many of your patients as you would if you were doing general medicine.

I'm lucky in that I don't have patients who are very ill. I'm very accepting of things the way they are and I'm not going to change things. There are very few things that happen in life that can be changed. So you go with the flow. What's meant to happen will happen and you deal with it. You adjust to it as best you can and go forward.

Communication with patients and staff is a big issue. In a hospital or a clinic I do that easily with the nurses and social workers. I had a patient recently with lung cancer and he's in real pain. Sometimes new residents and other docs have biases against giving people adequate analgesia. I don't care if he gets addicted. A lot of times maybe the oncologist has a different mind-set about patients and their comfort. You know you're dealing with a patient in a terminal or end-stage disease. Making the patient comfortable and pain free is keeping things going, the status quo. It's what's important and I think a lot of times it's the oncologist who has to sort of communicate that.

Chemotherapy works for some things. Is life being prolonged? Hopefully it is but for a lot of things it isn't. There's a group in Switzerland that's developing something that has to do with breast cancer, with the evaluation of quality of life issues in regard to giving chemotherapy and giving life expectancy. A whole system is trying to evaluate if what we're doing is really beneficial or not. It's very tough. Most of the big chemotherapy regimens don't increase survival very much—maybe a month or two. You give chemotherapy and see what happens. You give the best you have. If the patient responds very well, you go with it. If the patient doesn't respond and doesn't seem to be getting better, and the toxicity is bad, you stop. You don't push it to a point where you're building excesses of toxicity unless you're going to cure someone.

As to dealing with the family, that depends on the level of sophistication of the person. If the patient were relatively sophisticated and decently intelligent, I would tend to be much more honest with the family. Sometimes families run away. For most of the patients I see in the clinic the families are supportive. On the other hand, I had a patient who died of metastatic breast cancer, 36 or 38 years old, with children, who was in the hospital for months. I don't think I ever saw her husband visit her in the hospital except for the day before she died, when she was at the end stage. I've heard from nurses and from my wife, who's a nurse, that men tend to run. If their wives get sick, men tend to run. There are very few times when I've see a man deserted by his family, but there are many times when I've seen women deserted by theirs.

There are ethical differences between letting go and euthanasia. Strong ethical differences. Forget medicine, I'm talking ethics. There's a big difference between letting something natural happen and stopping them from doing anything to try to prevent that, which is a passive role, than from taking an active role. Being passively involved is very different from being actively involved, being an actor in causing something to occur, which is what euthanasia is. There's a big ethical difference. I would do everything to keep the patient comfortable. Pain control and everything else. I think hospices are great places. They're designed with one thing in mind: you have a patient with an end stage disease and whatever time they have to maximize their comfort and try to keep them from being uncomfortable and unhappy. It's perfect. As an oncologist there's a time and a place when you stop and say, "No more treatment. You're at a course in your illness when there are no real clear benefits. It's time to stop." This is as important as trying to prolong life. As an oncologist who's been trying to treat and prolong life, you switch hats, if you will, and come to the point where you're no longer going to try to prolong life but to maximize comfort.

If you look at doctors in general, and oncologists just as much, we probably have higher job satisfaction than any group of people in this country. I know that no matter what, I enjoy dealing with patients. I enjoy trying to help people and that's the bottom line. It's trying to make a difference, to help someone, make them live longer, feel better, be there a little for them. Oncologists have a high rate of burnout. A 50- or 55-year-old oncologist thinks he old. It has a high burnout rate because it's really intense. There's no question that there's a toll. You have to protect yourself from the patients. Don't get too close. If you start taking things very personally you can go crazy. I think oncologists learn coping mechanisms. It's easy to feel inadequate. You have all these patients who are sicker than hell, but you're willing to deal with it. You're not going to change reality. The reality is the patient is going to die no matter what you do. It's a lot better to die four years later than two years. If you can give someone two extra years with reasonable quality of life, it's worth doing.

It sounds like a great idea for physicians to show more compassion and empathy with a patient, but I don't know if it's even done. You have to balance your time. If you can find the time, good, but what you have to do takes 10 to 12 hours a day. An extra half-hour is an extra half-hour that you end up not seeing your bed or your children. They see little enough of their families as it is and they want to spend as much time as they can with them. The sad reality is that I haven't been out there. I don't know. If you're too busy and have to avoid something, it's easiest to avoid the things that are unpleasant.

Physicians not speaking to each other about death and dying may be because it brings up very personal issues. It's a touchy subject and they have their own ways of dealing with it. People have different coping mechanisms, including physicians, and they don't need anything more. On various occasions they go to their partners. The oncology group cries on each other's shoulders from time to time about patients who broke their hearts. I don't know that there should be a support group for physicians, but you need to have someone you're close to, another oncologist or whoever, to unbend a little. That's important.

Being on this job has changed me somewhat. I'm sometimes a little less sympathetic to people's minor problems. Like someone complaining about something that's total garbage, some minor thing, compared to what I've seen and what's out there. I think I'm a little more cynical now, or maybe jaded.

One of the things I'd like to see changed in this field is the attitude of a lot of people toward patients with cancer, because they're discriminated against. There's a stigma attached to these patients, which makes it hard for them to go on with their lives. I don't think people are uncompassionate, but there should be more of an acceptance, that sometimes, that's just the way it is. When patients are better and can go on with their jobs, a lot of times they get dead-ended because of the stigma that's attached to them.

If I had all the money in the world and didn't have to earn a living, I'd probably do something similar to what I'm doing now. Nothing dramatically different. I might do more research in the clinic and not go into private practice, which is what I want to do and probably will do. I'm very happy. I like what I'm doing and I have no huge desire to do something radically different. I'm happy.

* * *

Dr. Richards described the communicative and behavioral issues surrounding his death-related experiences in a thoughtful, albeit pragmatic and largely emotionally free fashion. I always wondered if this was how he actually approached his work and interactions with his patients as a form of coping strategy.

Unfortunately I have not been able to locate Dr. Richards. My understanding is that he is now practicing oncology in a medical group down south.

DR. BELL

My basic belief is that medicine is about people. If you don't like people, and you don't want to care for people, you don't want to work with people; you're in the wrong field. That's my basic belief. Coping with people is not a problem for me because I enjoy being with them. I enjoy spending time with them. But what I see around me isn't always pleasant. But I'm hopeless, helpless so to speak. I think there's very little I can do to change the way my colleagues address these situations.

I didn't choose medicine as a profession. During my senior year in college I took an examination in one of my zoology courses and the class average was 33. I scored a 67 on that exam, and it was such a phenomenal score that I was summoned by the chief of the department who wanted to know what my future plans were. I told him I had planned to continue and work toward a doctor's degree in parasitology. He told me to think seriously about going to medical school. He said, "I think it would afford you a happy existence. One of the things I feel you should be concerned about is that, no matter how bright you are, no matter how well you achieve in parasitology, someone with an MD degree will always be your boss, will always be telling you what to do." He asked me to spend another year there then offered to get me a position at the University of California, San Francisco. Later than spring when it was much too late to apply to medical school, a friend told me to speak with his father who was the dean of one of the two predominantly minority medical schools in the country. The next thing knew I was a freshman in medical school.

I went into medicine simply as a student with intense intellectual curiosity, not on a humanitarian or business basis. Doctor's can only do two things, really. They can help people to feel better, or they can help them to live longer. That's what medicine is all about. So naturally now that I'm in the field my job is to help people. But that is not why I studied medicine. I enjoyed the challenge of medical school tremendously but it didn't prepare me for the job I'm doing now. Medical students shy away from courses in nutrition, psychiatry, psychology, sociology, and patient interactions because they are all gung-ho scientists. They want to do complicated things, procedural things. They get very excited treating electrolyte imbalance or surgical conditions. I'm not sure you can teach interpersonal communication. There are some schools that place more emphasis on patient-doctor interaction such as Georgetown and Columbia. And I used to hear nurses say, "You can tell a doctor from Georgetown." But in some medical schools patient care is now unregulated, and the emphasis is on scientific endeavors, publishing, research, and grant getting.

I think as medicine is evolving in this country the powers that be are going to begin to look hard at how money's being spent, and they're going to see that more time and effort need to be placed on primary care patients. You see, primary care in medicine is not a glamorous area, and many people, at least in years gone by, who enrolled in medicine thought it was a glamorous specialty. Many prospective medical students tell you "I want a decent income so that I can raise my family, and educate them properly." Some will tell you, "I want to be a researcher." And a minority of them will tell you, "I'm doing this because I really want to help people." But I don't really believe them, if you want my honest opinion, because, for example, a new medical school was established a little more than a decade ago, the Sophie Davis Biomedical program at CCNY, and the purpose of the program was to train doctors for the inner city. I would say 90 percent of those physicians practice everywhere except the inner city. I guess they don't find an intellectual challenge, an intellectual satisfaction, in working in the inner city.

You have to understand the medical infrastructure. If you applied to one of our premier medical institutions and told them you just wanted to take care of patients, you probably would be rejected. You would never get into medical school. If you applied to one of the top-level internships and told them that was your purpose, you wouldn't get a slot. The chairman of the department of medicine tells the students, "Don't worry about the patients. Get some bench experience in. You can always catch up on the patients later." He was the chief of medicine at one of our medical schools in New York City. Sure, it's sad.

I'm a little unique compared to some of the people with whom I work. For example, a couple of years ago I had a few patients in the hospital whose illnesses were AIDS related. I used to wait until the end of the day, between 7 and 8 P.M. and I used to go around, sit on their beds and talk to them. I'd come in on Saturdays or Sundays when everything was quiet. Mostly I talked with them, not about the illness, but I let them talk to me about their lives and their broken dreams, and about the terrible things their relatives were doing to them, and so forth and so on. I talked to them more or less as friends, or acquaintances about their medical problems, particularly your patients with advanced malignancies for which there's no suitable chemotherapy. There are people who would say to me, "Are you out of your mind? You're coming back here at 7 o'clock to talk to these people. Don't you have better things to do on weekends except come in to see patients?" They think it's quite odd. But it's something I particularly have enjoyed, and continue to enjoy. I talk to those patients who I think are receptive and who don't have large families, who have very few visitors and who I feel need extra support.

As a medical student I found it extremely difficult to cope with children with cancer and children with leukemia. As a matter of fact, as a medical student I made one decision: that pediatrics was a field I could never go into because I have such deep feelings for little kids. But with AIDS patients I recognize that we're all mortal, and they may be a little younger than patients with cancer, but I don't really have difficulty dealing with them. I don't feel any differences. We have patients with malignant disease in the third and fourth decade, so it isn't that difficult.

In terms of an overview, I think the approach to malignant diseases as well as AIDS in this country is misguided in the sense that tremendous sums of money are spent to correct things that could have been prevented. For example, cancer of the lung and cancer of the colon we spend millions of dollars, hundreds of millions of dollars a year, treating patients for whom you can only anticipate marginal improvement in life, a few weeks, at the cost of significant adverse effects from the drugs. Whereas if a small part of this money was spent on educating children about the evils of tobacco and alcohol beginning in elementary school, it would be much more effective both in terms of morbidity and mortality, and cost. I think that AIDS is a totally preventable disease and the education effort for AIDS falls far short of what it might have been, considering the money and the expertise that's available in this country. For example, I recall a few years ago the son of one of the leading physicians in New York City succumbed to AIDS. He was an Ivy League graduate and at the beginning of the AIDS epidemic. He visited his local internist to talk about it and to find out what he needed to do to sort of reduce or minimize the risk of developing AIDS, and was told by the physician to cut down on his sexual encounters. He asked the doctor what he meant and he said, "Cut down from 15 to 20 partners a week to three or four." This is very bad information for any person to give, but this patient went to a source he thought was reliable, but got the kind of advice that could cost him his life.

I had a patient who had a heart attack when I was an intern, 26 or 27 years ago, and she knitted me two pairs of socks, which I still wear. It's unbelievable that after all these years I still have them. But every time I got a break on my internship, and there was so much work to be done in those days, we used to do our own blood counts, urinalysis, type and cross match, the whole bit. But every time I had a spare moment I used to go back and plop down on the bed beside her, and she would knit and we would talk, and she would tell me about her childhood. She was good for me; I was good for her. I really got her through the difficult period following her heart attack. I didn't really do anything for the heart attack, as the heart will heal itself, but I made her hospital stay, and I think her passion for continued life, important.

The most important communication that takes place is that between the doctor and the patient, particularly if the patient is terminally ill, and that's my major focus. Families bring in all sorts of complexities, which could take days and days to try to unravel. It's so complex. There are no simple answers. There are families whose primary concern is that the uncle's $60,000 in the bank not be spent before we can get our hands on it. Their prime concern is not to let uncle go into a nursing home, not to let Uncle come back home, or any place where any of this money can be spent. Stop all therapy and let Uncle die, or put uncle in a hospice. Those are the kinds of conflicts and problems we deal with. We deal with people who have been hating each other all their lives, and the wife can't wait to see the husband die, and the husband can't wait to see the wife die. You deal with people who feel that, "Oh, I'm so glad it's him not me." It's a very difficult situation. Families have motives, the likes of which you cannot imagine. Patients will tell you, for example, "She's got two lawyers, she's trying to sell the apartment. So even if I do get out of the hospital, I've got no apartment to go to. They've already started to squabble over my possessions and I'm not dead yet." I find it easier to deal with the patient than with the families, see; the families' hearts are not always in the right place. That doesn't mean there aren't some families that are devoted to the relatives, but all of these hidden hostilities that have been there over the years seem to surface when a patient is terminally ill. The wives come and say, "Doctor, don't tell him I told you, but whatever you do, don't let him come home. He wants to come home but it's too much for me. I really just can't do it, I mean it's too much of a burden. Please don't tell him I said it." That's the kind of thing we deal with. I don't think the family is always the best advocate for the patient. That's why I think the communication should be between the patient and doctor.

A patient will tell you, for example, "Don't tell him that I'm dying. Just between the two of us, I don't want them to know." I'm very honest and up front with patients. I tell them precisely what their diagnosis is. I give them a very good idea about what we can and cannot do. I tell them very early on that there will come a time when you will no longer be able to care for yourself, and I would rather begin to talk about that now, rather than later. It's not something I hide or hold back 'til the last minute. I find them very accepting.

The way the nurse's fit into this communication process may be an area that needs to be looked at very carefully, because what we do is frequently not coordinated. What they're telling them may be different from what I'm telling them, and we don't do this as a group. Many times the social worker or nurse will say "Can we meet at 3 o'clock, and we'll go and speak to Jack so-and-so, and tell him about going to the hospice because he's reluctant, and he says he's not going." And perhaps this is wrong on my part, but I'll slip by and see Jack alone and then I'll give them both a ring and I'll say, "Well, Jack's okay now. He's relaxed. He's ready to go to the hospice." I find that I'm much more effective solo than I am in a group. I find that one of my talents seems to be that patients immediately perceive that I am there for them, and they tend to trust me, and they will do things for me that they won't do for anybody else on the service.

I don't think it's necessary for the patient to hear what's going to happen from ten different people. The patient usually identifies with one or more members of the medical team. For example, my patients if I'm out of town or if something should happen and they go to another hospital, they will tell the doctor, "Here is Dr. Ballard's number. Nothing can be done until you talk to him." Even if the nurse and a doctor or a group got together and they spoke to the patient about his situation and would say, "You have colon cancer; it's spread beyond the confines of the bowel. We can't really cure you but we can control it." Well each time you see the patient there might be a slight change in status which you need to go over with him. It would be kind of impossible after each change to again call in the nurse, and the social worker, and the psychologists, and again go over all those changes. You just couldn't do it.

I never feel that I put up a wall, but I don't get involved emotionally with most people I know, even outside the field of medicine. I get involved with my patients' problems and I assist them as best I can. For example, a few days ago my mother's sister called me and said she had vaginal bleeding. I said you probably have cancer of the uterus, and I want you to go, first thing tomorrow and have a gynecological examination. You should have your uterus removed as soon as possible.

She followed through. She had a cancer of the uterus. It was removed and she was cured. But I didn't lay awake all that night, or I didn't get terribly emotionally caught up in the fact that my aunt has a cancer. I don't know how to describe that. I wasn't any more emotionally involved than I would be if a patient came to me and had the same situation.

I went with my father once to see his doctor some years ago. His doctor said, "Well, aren't you too young to be in oncology? I mean, isn't that difficult for a young person to deal with?" And I kind of smiled and said, "You see, for me death is the ultimate." All of us will eventually get there, and I think that after a person reaches a certain few decades in life, he's at least had a chance to know what life is like. It's not nice if they die before they're 80, 90 years old, but it's something I can deal with. But I find the younger age groups more difficult. I don't see, for example, a 33-year-old woman with a lovely nine-year-old daughter that's she's very much attached to, and she's dying from breast cancer. I don't know how I would deal with that. Our patient population is a little older. Many of them have cancers as a consequence of their own habits. Not that I hold that against them, but we don't have to deal much with their children.

At times patients employ a defense mechanism of believing the physician is capable of curing everything. I had a patient who had cancer of the stomach with widespread metastasis. He had been operated on, found to be inoperable, and eventually ended up here. He said, "Now doctor, be honest with me. If I have an incurable disease, there are a couple of things I need to know." He was Irish, and he said, "My mother lives in Ireland, in this little village, and if I'm going to die, I'd like to go back to Ireland and spend my last days with her. And there's a woman I've had a relationship with for the last 10 years here in Brooklyn, and . . . we've had a good relationship. I want to be able to bequeath some things to her. So these two things are very important to me, so I want you to let me know exactly where I stand." So I thought it was appropriate, I mean, I waited a few days, and I said, "Mr. McIntyre, let's go in the office. I'm gonna talk to you, and I need the blackboard." So I got the blackboard and I drew the stomach and I showed him the lesions on the stomach, and I showed him the metastasis in the liver in different places. I said, "This is where you are now." I said, "Remember that little conversation we had, you said you wanted to go back and spend time with your mother, and you wanted to do certain things with this woman? I think it's now time for you to begin to actually activate this process." And he looked at me and he says, "You know Doc, where I made my big mistake? I went to Brooklyn Jewish Hospital and they really didn't know how to cure the cancer. But I know you can do it. I know you are going to cure me." I say, "Now I've just explained to you what we have here, and I really can't." He says, "Look. You can do it. I know you can do it." We went through that conversation every few days until he died. That enabled him to survive in relative comfort his last few days. You never take a crutch away from a patient.

I don't know if you can teach kindness. For example, we gave a little luncheon for a nurse in oncology who was retiring. One of the other physicians said to me, "Well, I really don't think I should go." I said, "Why not?" He said, "Well, she's only a nurse, and why should I go? If I gave something, I wouldn't invite any nurses. Why should I waste my time going?" How could a person like this be kind to a patient? But we can't weed these people out. This person went to an Ivy League school, has a magna cum laude degree in science, and that's how he got into medical school. He got into medical school because he's capable of making good grades; that's how he gets a MD, because nobody was concerned about the humanistic aspect.

There are things I would have much rather done than be a physician. I would have enjoyed nothing more than let's say, being a concert artist, playing in a symphony orchestra, being a writer. These are particular things I would have enjoyed enormously. I wanted to be in the State Department. I think I would be very good as a diplomat. But I have no regrets. I've thoroughly enjoyed medicine. I'm one person who gets up in the morning and can hardly wait to get to work. I look forward to each day with anticipation. I haven't tired yet. I complain sometimes, but I really enjoy it.

*   *   *

Dr. Bell was the first doctor I interviewed. His reasons for becoming a doctor and how he has realistically communicated and managed his life over the years while interacting with terminal patients, families and peers is at the heart of this narrative.

As an oncology sales representative Dr. Bell often invited me into his office to talk about his love of classical music and European travel. He always took an interest in my life and career as well. Without hesitation he accepted my invitation to be interviewed.

Dr. Bell is still the assistant director of hematology and oncology at a prominent teaching hospital in the New York metropolitan area. I'm indebted to him for his encouragement

and advisement in pursuing the idea to do a book on oncology
health professionals.

DR. JONES, ONCOLOGY FELLOW

One of the most common questions I am asked is, "How do you do that?" and "How do you handle the death?" I always thought the question was, "How could you do that?" You know that it is such a terrible, difficult thing to do. The more people ask me, I'm getting the impression they're not asking me for that reason. They're asking me to give them some sort of magical answers so that they can handle it too. I always thought that they were just curious about how I could do what I do. But, I think it's much more self-serving. They want to know what is this secret. I can't obviously give that to them. I give sort of a pat answer about how it's challenging, it's interesting, it's difficult, yes, but I enjoy it.

I have been an oncology fellow for eleven months. Before that I was in hematology for a year. I found I liked working with people as opposed to working in a laboratory all the time. The thing about hematology and oncology is that I spent good portions of time with pathologies, with surgeons and obstetricians, as well as neurosurgeons and neurologists. I see all fields, all types of surgery. I deal with all organ processes and I can learn from everybody. That's another reason why I like hematology and oncology. Blood and cancer affect all parts of the body.

Now that I have done both I find that oncology would be more challenging. I like the idea of maybe having a brain cancer case on one day, and a colon cancer on the next, or a breast cancer case. It's more diverse than hematology. Most people don't have a grasp of hematology. People have trouble viewing blood as an organ system. It's not like it doesn't have a shape to it; it transverses the whole body. With oncology, if you have breast cancer, it's a lump in the breast. It's very anatomical. It has to come out. You have to get chemotherapy. So it's just that the challenge in oncology is so diverse. The challenge in oncology is finding out what the problem is and then sometimes finding if we can get a cure. A lot of times there may not be and that's one of the things about oncology. I can't give anyone quantities but I can give them quality, make the pain go away and relieve symptoms. There are a lot of cancers that are not curable, but again, sometimes we can prolong life. Sometimes we can prolong it long enough with a good quality of life that makes it worthwhile. I think, unfortunately, that a lot of patients' lives are prolonged longer than they should be, and the quality of life isn't there.

The way I handle a patient getting worse depends on a lot of things, such as the age of the patient, and what they have. But you can't let yourself get bogged down into it. You have to desensitize yourself to the process. I think desensitization begins in medical school, in the anatomy labs when you see the dead bodies. You know it's not a human. It was a human, but it's not someone you know, moving and doing things, eating and going to work. So you forget those human characteristics and use it as an object, to learn anatomy. And from there you go on. When your patients get sick and die, if you were to react like a family member or even a friend, you would be lost. So when problems come up and you're having some disagreement with another service or with other doctors about patient care and it's not going the way you want it to, you can't get all worked up about it. Because it will cause you to have peptic ulcers, or you'll have a stroke, go crazy, or you'll just never be able to handle it. You'll have a breakdown, a nervous breakdown.

We have all types of words, like desensitization, and thought processes to separate the patient from ourselves, and their death process. I think desensitization is necessary because as I said, without it you would not be able to survive. I guess it's like how anyone becomes desensitized if your are hit with something enough. Like if you have an allergy to something and they give that substance in small quantities repeatedly, so your body can build up a defense mechanism. It's the same thing with all these dying people. If you see it so much it lays another brick for the wall, on and on, so that they are actually helping you in a way, every patient that dies. From the onset the initial thought process is work up the patient. You want to do what is absolutely necessary. You don't want to be doing things that are not necessary or just for the patient's comfort. Go full blast ahead, gung ho, find out what's happening, how extensive the disease is, how terminal is the patient. Then you say we're not going to get anywhere with any type of chemo-therapy or radiation or surgery.

You can work as hard as you can and do as much as you can and things are not going to work the way you want them to. You have to get used to it. With all your good intentions people die or something can go wrong, terribly wrong. In the forties, fifties, and even into the sixties, the doctor's word was law. It's not happening now and it's good and bad. People have trouble realizing that we're not godlike, we're going to be subject to the same pitfalls and insecurities as other people, like making wrong decisions or just being so tired one day, not being able to do what we need to do. Or something else happens to our family that we have to take care of. It's not possible to give 100 percent to every patient all the time. Helping doesn't mean curing. Making life better is very important.

When I first experienced a patient death was in my internship at City College Hospital. My internship was very difficult, because in the space of a month I had eight deaths, which is astronomical. I thought it was me. But the thing was, I then went from August to February without any deaths. So all the other interns pulled out maybe one or two a month. It's the luck of the draw. You could get somebody who is dead in the emergency ward, or just about to die, they get committed to you and they die the next morning. That happens. And I felt that maybe there was something I could have done. I felt terrible. Did I feel guilty? Sure. I would go back and re-read things, and keep on going over things in my mind. I was totally scared. And then people would say, "Oh, it's nothing. This is what's going to happen. This is how it goes." You can work as hard as you can and do as much, and it's just not going to, you know, things are not going to work the way you want them. And you have to get used to it. That was probably one of the most important things I learned during my internship.

One of the most important things that helped me initially with the internship, dealing with death and my residency was running. I would run. And a lot of times every step I took was the neck of a patient, or another resident, or an attendee, or the guy in the elevator who didn't want to take me up one flight with a patient because it was 5:01 and he was going home. That really helped. What it wound up doing was releasing a lot of pressure and tension. I also became a good long distance runner. I could almost gauge how bad a week I had by the number of miles I had run that week.

Chemotherapy does help patients. It's the best we have right now. Well, it does have problems. That's why research in all fields is so important because in the future something else may come out to be better, or maybe a combination of chemo and something else. But to abandon chemo now and put all our eggs in the basket of the future is not going to help the people who are alive today. We have an outpatient chemo room in every hospital. People come in and out, get their chemo with not many problems at all. Although there are problems, it's gotten much better in the last twenty-five years. You put someone on speed for a day or six or eight hours, so then they don't even remember getting the chemo. The growth factors are so important now. They bring up white counts. In the past the majority of people died from the side effects of chemo, which lower white cell counts and platelets. They bled out or they got infected. We can prevent these things now and that's great. If you give women with breast cancer a cycle of drugs and compare them with other women with breast cancer who receives nothing, the women receiving chemo for six months will last longer and not have the cancer come back, than ones who gets nothing. Maybe you feel a little miserable, or a lot miserable for four or six months, but you have a life span of seven years, as opposed to not getting anything and dying in two to three years from metastatic breast cancer. Strangely enough, I had ten new breast cancer patients within the last two weeks of which surgery was curative. I have to make absolutely certain they will get chemotherapy for the next number of months. If I didn't I am sure one those ten women would have a recurrence of the cancer, without the chemo. So by giving it, even if you save one woman, it's certainly worthwhile.

The people I have known who have died have been very old or very sick, but they were not close to me. Death came peacefully and it was natural and expected. I have never been to a funeral of a relative or a close friend, where it was a shock to have them die. I have never had a direct family member die so I don't' know what it's like. Obviously, I have seen a lot of people die but it's tough when you have a seven-year-old kid who gets hit by a car. That's tough and that much harder to explain.

If you're seventy years old and you have lung cancer, bad as that is, it's not so bad to say "You know, okay, you have lung cancer and we can't fix it. But we can make you comfortable, make sure you understand what's happened, and answer all your questions." It's much harder to say that to a six or seven year old who has leukemia. That I find hard. I sometimes look at pediatric oncologists and hematologists and I don't' know how they walk in to a seven year old and try to explain that to them, or to the parents of the seven year old.

I was very lucky. The first time I had to tell that a family member had died was to a wife. She said, "Thank God. He was suffering. I'm so relieved. We all expected it, thank you very much. You know, you've been more than helpful." I was waiting for the worst and when she did that, I was so happy. It started off really well, but it's also been awful. I have had family members who freak out and jump on the body of the person who died, start beating them, come back to me and plead and beg to get the heart beating again. But as I said, I was very fortunate the first time it worked out well.

Death is part of all our lives. It's going to happen to every one of us, and it happens to a lot of people we know. And most people, obviously, look at death with a negative aspect. It's not necessarily bad to die. It may actually be okay. You cannot be here all the time. When I see people die and other people think that's terrible, or another doctor says, "Well, look, the patient died," I don't look at it that way at all. I just think that death is part of this process and that they move on. And maybe they do move on to something else, but that's like getting into philosophical or theological connotations. I don't think I have to do that. I just believe this is how it's supposed to go. It's like moving on a line, from A to B and somewhere in that line, there is a mark, and that's death. And I just happen to be right before that line, okay? Sometimes we can move that point of death back farther on that line and sometimes we can't, and that's fine. You know, we can try and if we can do it, we do it, and if we can't, that's okay. As I said, the idea is to communicate with the patient what they have, what I can try to do for them, what may happen. You know the possibilities. We can't predict.

You can't get locked into cures. I never give patients times. If I said you had six months and your live three, the family's going to come back and accuse me of gypping them out of three months. If I said six months and the patient lasted years, the family will think I'm an idiot. I can't predict the future, but I can predict maybe a short time in the future. If somebody comes in with a metastatic disease, that doesn't mean they are going to die, but if you have a terminal disease, I still will not tell them for the simple reason that everything, like test grades, is on a curve. If the cancer had eroded into a major blood vessel, and if it opens that blood vessel they could die; they could die in the space of moments. I will tell them that they have a terminal disease and that they probably won't last long, but I can't predict how long they are going to last.

I have no trouble talking about death with patients and family members because I do it all the time. I think it's because we do it all the time and I may be better at it than the general medical services because they don't have to do it. If you're an internist, and they see extremely important diseases like cardiac disease or high blood pressure or diabetes, and they can be death-threatening illnesses also, but those things can be managed for years, whereas for the most of my patients that is not the case. So the internists have much more trouble dealing with it because they don't see it as much. But as I said, I see it all the time so I have no trouble talking to the family, to the patient, doing it more than once if necessary, and just bang the thing through.

It's classic. It's one of the things I see a lot. It's very strange. It's funny you picked up on that. When someone is terminal the doctors who have been around along time abandon ship. Unfortunately, it's their problem. They have trouble coping. And, then sometimes the oncologist comes in at that moment, or the hematologist and they get stuck, because they're the only ones there and everything falls on them. The other thing that's sometimes even worse is that the doctors say we're going to really go. So instead of disappearing at this moment, they order every test, they do every removal possible, and that makes it even worse. Part of the idea of knowing how to do this is to pull back. Letting go. Sometimes it's even worse dealing with those physicians because they want to run everything. And if the patient doesn't know what's happening and they go along with all this, it makes it even worse.

I mentioned before that I didn't have any experience with a close friend or relative who had died, but I did have one experience with someone I had known only for six months, a young man who died of cancer. The house staff and the residents didn't know that I knew this person outside the hospital and there were a lot of comments made when the person was dying that you would not make in front of family or a friend, to whom it would be offensive. One of the terms people use here is intubation, which is putting the tube down the throat, which he refused, but he'll go for the "electric cardio." So one of the residents said, " Well, why don't we just put a radio on his chest." When they were taking this person away, the guy from the morgue came up and put the body on the side of the hallway and walked toward the nurse's station. There were people around, so he turned back to the body and says, "Don't go anywhere." Everybody laughed. He was not a physician. He just rolls dead bodies around all day. That may be his defense mechanism. The point that I got from this is you have to be very careful what you say, where you say it, who is around, and who is behind you, because it can make a difference. Sometimes it's very difficult to be able to consciously hold your tongue. You don't know whose family members or friends are around or the doctors may know the patient in a different way. So you always have to be very careful and choose your words carefully. I didn't see the person from the morgue as being disrespectful to the person who's dead; it didn't bother me, but if the resident did it, that may be questionable. It's just something that you have to consciously make an effort to remember at all times, and that can bring on a lot of stress too, just having to do that. It is the responsibility of my colleagues to make each other aware of this.

It would be better if it didn't happen. It's not that it's wrong, it's that these people, again, are human beings and they're going to be subject to making these mistakes. They probably make them for the most part unconsciously. I know the doctors here are very conscientious. They are very respectful when talking directly to the patient or family members. They are not going to be flippant. It's just that, you're in the midst of running a code or something, things may be said or done that you're just not thinking about. Maybe it's more of an auto pilot thing. It's hard. It's just another thing you have to learn. It's not in a medical book anywhere or a textbook.

I'll give you another good example. When I was an intern a woman came in with a huge breast cancer. Big, big mass, lacerations, bleeding, infected mass siting on her chest. Didn't speak at all. Just bounced up and around on the bed. We went in and didn't even look at the face; we looked at the patient's lesion. The second year resident went, "Wow." And, I whistled. An attendee was there. So we examined the patient and then went back out. The attendee ripped us apart. She said, "I don't care if the woman was in a coma. That is not the way to treat human beings, especially when they are awake. Even if she has no idea what you've done. You cannot do things like that." I mean she was really pissed, and she made life very difficult for us for about a week. So, I remembered that. When you see terrible things on patients, you have to make sure that you keep, sort of, a poker face. And if you're shocked or disgusted, you have to back away from it consciously for a minute, so that you don't upset the patient. And that can be difficult, too. As far as being taught she laid it out in front of all the other doctors and nurses, very loud, that if we ever did that again, we would in big trouble. It was the embarrassment factor that I remember, too. It's something I will not forget, and I'll make sure that I don't whistle in front of a patient like that. Good learning experience. Again, I don't think it's in a textbook anywhere.

The fear of death, the denial of death, and communicating effectively in relationship to the death process is largely cultural. I mean, the best example right off the top of my head is that there is a very large oriental population here. The Asians, by and large, not always, have specifically stated that they do not want the patient to know the disease. And it can be difficult for us because here, legally, we're responsible to the patient. We're not supposed to be doing things to the patient, or withholding information, so you sort of get caught in a trap. I've found that when the oriental patients and their families do not speak any English that it is fine. I'm willing to bet that the overwhelming majority of patients understand anyway. They have a sense of what is happening. They don't want to know the minutiae, which is fine. But the kids do, and a lot of times they make the decisions, whether to continue or stop treatment. Which is fine, too. I know certain oriental populations don't want people dying at home because the spirit will then be trapped in the house, which maybe the opposite of what we would like. We like the home hospice care where people can die around their families, in their own bed, which sounds nicer to me, but if that's what they want, that's fine. So people will hold their parents or whomever at home until they're really sick, then bring them in the ER and let it go there, and they'll wind up dying here. That's, that's okay, too. I'm trying to think, I would say that the better educated you are, probably, you're going to be little bit better at handling the death process. Certainly the older your are the better you handle it. It's a funny misconception that a lot of people will believe, "Oh, we can't tell grandma, because she'll never be handle the bad news." Grandparents handle bad news much better than their grandkids. Probably, because they've been through a lot more their whole life, so their use to it. I've learned also that you can be very straightforward with older people. They'll say, "Look, I'm eighty years old, you know, this wasn't going to go on forever, and I understand that." Where it becomes more difficult is the 17-year-old guy or the 25-year-old woman. I haven't really seen that one sex handles it better than the other does consistently. I'd say it's individual. I think women have an advantage that they're able to articulate more. And, that it's socially sanctioned for them to cry, and to release, whereas men don't and probably hold it in more. It's like the old stereotypes. Women will meet together, have bull sessions, and cry; men will go to a bar and drink and be very sullen. So I think women are actually luckier in that respect, but that may be a sexist attitude. Different populations will respond differently to death, but I don't think it's teachable as how to respond and maybe it shouldn't be.

You can get lost and be butting your head against the wall as far as the institution and its bureaucracy is concerned. It sometimes gets very frustrating. You may request a CAT-scan for a patient but the radiologist may not believe it is indicated, although he or she may be very well trained and very knowledgeable. But it's more than that. They've never met the patient or they don't understand the indication. Maybe the patient wants to go to Puerto Rico for one last time and has to get the CAT-scan before he or she can go. I know they're backed up but they'll say, "This is the rule, this is how we're going to play it." So, again, you butt your head against the wall. Everyday there's a hurdle. It could be any department. It could be talking with the surgeons; it could be something as simple as needing someone to give them chemo. The surgeons don't have time. It could be that the patient doesn't have a Medicaid card, so the secretary at the front desk, at the OR clinic doesn't want to register the patient. They missed the bus, they got up late, or they did something else the night before. All these things you just have to take them in stride, but it can rally drive you crazy, and you go home mad. It's part of the whole job. God forbid life should be so boring.

There's a couple of ways to look at how I find meaning in an environment where I see death on an everyday basis. You know, like, there are few people in the world that can do the things that Michael Jordan can do. Obviously, this is nowhere near like that. But it is like that, in that we do something that the majority of people can't do. I'm proud of that. You are helping people and a lot of people can't do this. I'm very happy about that, and this helps in all aspects of life. Because of what's happening here, when I get outside I appreciate everything much more. I see green in the trees, I hear the calm when there is no noise. I can stop and slow down, sort of pull back for a moment and just take that moment as just that moment in time, and not just let everything keep on going, going; like people sitting on alpha waves all day and just, basically getting through life. I think that's when life becomes really real. When these terrible things happen to people, whereas the rest of their lives sometimes can be gray, so now it becomes very colorful, when these tragic things happen to them, and it doesn't even have to be cancer. It can be a car accident. Since I see that all the time, I remember that a lot more. So, I make sure that those other times I try and keep them in perspective. My work is very important, but outside of work is very important, too, going out with friends, dating. In the next year or two I will be setting out my future for the long term and that's important. As I said, the challenge is here and I enjoy it. Working with people is a lot of fun. Again, it's hard working with patients. Hard meaning it can be difficult because they have such difficult diseases, but it's a challenge and I like doing it.

I've always liked the field of science and if I were not in medicine, I guess I could be doing something in physics or chemistry. It's hard to put yourself in another job if you're already so well ensconced in a job. But, you know, everybody fantasizes about becoming some great ball player or something like that, we all have those fantasies, but this is what I wanted and that's fine. I'll just continue from here.

*   *   *

Dr. Jones' narrative gives readers another perspective on what it is like for a new, young oncology doctor to treat and care for people who are dying.

In the early months of 1999, Dr. Jones greeted me warmly in his office. We filled in eight years of living in sixty minutes. As an early supporter of this book, he was happy to hear of its impending publication. Since graduating medical school, Dr. Jones has been working steadily in a well-known city hospital. He spoke excitedly about the changes in his life. He married four years ago, with first child on the way, and is proudly involved in cutting edge hematology/oncology research.

DR. AHMED

I remember the first time this was asked to me, "Why did you get into medicine"? When I went for the interview for medical school I said I had some interest in medicine right from childhood. I said I enjoyed medicine in order to work with people and that it was what I wanted to do for a long time. No, my parents were not in medicine, but they said when I was very little I had an interest in medicine. You know I used to play doctor and when I was in college this is what I felt I had to be. What I found appealing was the enjoyment doctors got out of what they were doing. I felt that this is what I wanted to be.

I've been both a hematologist and oncologist for over twenty years. I went to school in India. Hematology malignancy used to be considered a royal malignancy. There was a lot more interest in taking care of those patients from the point of view of the physician, and from a teaching and research point of view also because what you were learning from there became the basis of the treatment of the solid tumors. So, in that sense hematological malignancies were kind of a royal malignancy, and in fact they still hold a little special place because there's a lot more you could see. You look at those malignancies in the smear in cases of the solid tumors. You depend on the pathologist to give you the diagnosis. You see with them, but you're depending on them to show you what it is. With the hematologic tumors you are the expert.

I think now there's been a lot more progress in therapeutic results of the solid tumors. The solid tumors are much more frequent; particularly malignancies like lung, breast, and colon. A lot more attention is being paid both at the research and clinical level. You know I'm sure, for example the oncologist would say that lymphoma is an interesting disease but your bread and butter is the breast carcinoma, as you see many more patients of breast carcinoma than lymphoma.

Yes, to an extent I do have a preference. I'm much more knowledgeable in certain malignancies, like breast cancer. You see I'm more of an expert in that field. So, I have a certain preference for that as against other malignancies, partly because it is therapeutically treatable and you see the benefits if the patients do get better. That's satisfying, sure.

I didn't practice in India. I came here immediately after graduation. Multi-culturalism is a big issue. Well, yes I do feel it. There are different philosophies of medicine, communication, and coping with people who have life challenging illnesses. At one time, of course, when I was in medical school there was no teaching of communication. You didn't communicate with patients, you just dictate to patients. They never asked too many questions. They accepted anything; they didn't ask what your diagnosis was or what the treatment you are giving is. Patients expressed a lot of faith in doctors.

I think that has changed quite a bit. I find now that in oncology you have to sit down with the patient, explain the whole chemotherapy, and explain what you're going to do. This is a given. They ask a lot more questions, and still many times patients would say, "But, you didn't tell me this or you didn't tell me that." And you know that you told that to the patient. And especially in oncology, the patients are all the time denying themselves about the disease they have, so they are somehow obscuring or forgetting about what was told them. One of the things I would say is that, yeah, there was a lot less communication between doctor and patients then, and now there is more. No, no there was absolutely no teaching regarding communication in medical school.

Communication between physicians, family members, and patients has evolved over the last twenty years. I remember in 1968 when I was going into medicine and starting my practice here, communication was not a major thing. Why is this? Well, I think it has to be that patients are demanding it. Speaking to those patients you realized they became much more intelligent about their disease. They knew more about it from the media and other information regarding the body. So they were asking more questions. I remember, for example, we used to do bone marrows, tell the patient and we stuck the patient with the needle, just saying, "Turn on your side and we'll do a bone marrow," you know. It was about that simple, how little you would tell them. Of course now we have those informed consents. Even then we did it for the patient, and even now we do it for the patient, except that then we didn't explain to the patient why we were doing this. Without any explaining they, and all their family members, trusted the doctors about it.

Yeah it did feel cold and insensitive. But you always felt that you were doing the right thing for the patient. That was enough. And the patient had full faith in the doctors. Taking together those things, that was enough. Right, we were never intending to do anything wrong. You know when the patients give consent in deciding what should be done, it's just as important as your intentions of doing the right thing. So that's why I think right now full communication with the patient is important. In taking the consent, the doctor's bias plays a very important role. I mean, for example, if I want to give a certain treatment over another treatment, there are two choices and then we can say, " Let the patient make the choice." I could put the treatments in a way, you know, where the patient would accept the treatment I want, against the alternative treatment, because I've pumped up probably more benefits in one, a little more risk in the other. Uh, not all, but most physicians don't effectively communicate. Many complex reasons. Time certainly can be a factor, you know. It always takes time to explain to the patient how to understand what is going on. And you explain more, more questions arise on the part of the patient and family. How do I deal with it? Well, we could take a few cases. Like I had a woman last year and she had carcinoma of the ovary. She had two other doctors over the several months I was involved. She put a lot of faith in me, especially because the initial chemotherapy that I gave her made a response, and she felt very comfortable with the treatment and with my communications her family. So they were depending on me very much. I was explaining to both the patient and more particularly the family, that the number of cases for this disease is very small and a cure is not likely to be the case. We don't know how long she's going to live. She continued to be really comfortable with me until she relapsed and a time came that we were not able to offer her much therapy, except a supportive therapy in the terminal days when she developed some infections in the hospital.

Yes I did. I had a lot of difficulties with the family, emotionally. They were calling me and coming to see me again and again, "What's happening?" Finally, when the day came to speak with the patient I talked to both daughters and told them that things were not looking too good. I was letting it kind of get to me. She was crying. She just didn't know how to cope with it. And many times I find it important to have good experienced nurses with me in these situations. Like I have Bernice here, the nurses can sit down and talk to them for a longer time. So that helps because the support helps very much. The support is very crucial. In this case, Pat sat down with that family and she talked with them for quite some time. We had another nurse Susan who was also quite a bit involved with that. There were others who were sharing with me in the support of this family. The patient did die that night.

Well, of course, it is sad and hard for us, but the next day I did talk with the family about it. I explained to them about her, that we couldn't do any more than we were able to do. But I wanted to make sure the family had felt fully involved, that they did what they could, they were very supportive of me and had been very helpful to their mother. And I always feel this is very important. Many times I think the family members feel very guilty about not being able to do everything they could. For example, I was recently involved with a mother and her son, for about two years. She had many ups and downs and her son was fully involved in her care. He used to come to the hospital everyday and call many times. She was very sick and ICU. He was just pacing up and down in ICU and kept saying, "I hope I have done everything. I hope I have done everything right." So I asked him why do you keep feeling that, you've been there with her for two years and she knows that? "And you have done, you know everything to comfort her." One of the medical ICU nurses came over to him, and again, spoke to him about the same thing. He did feel somewhat comforted, but you know, as I say he was quite a bit broken up about it.

I'll give you another example. I had a woman with carcinoma of the lung. She had four sons, all young men, and her husband. The whole family, the five of them, was very much involved. She was a very strong woman in the family. She was hospitalized several times and responded initially very nicely to chemotherapy. She had an adeno carcinoma of the lung, which I looked up and pointed out to the family that all the literature will tell you that median survival is about six months. This lady, for whatever her reasons, had gone about two years with that disease. And the family's involvement was quite a bit, but they didn't feel happy that they had done everything on their part, that they could do. On the other hand, I kept pushing them that yes; you have all this support. Look at that she's gone two years with this disease. You have done much at home, you have done much in the hospital, you have spent a lot of time here. And you know, every time when she comes here you're with her. Many times two, three sons used to be there.

I wouldn't say that I feel guilty when I can't cure people. Yes, many times I do feel angry, frustrated that there's nothing out there. I always feel most of the time the patients don't want to die. They want to stay alive. A few families give up, but most of the time families don't give up, they want something done. Certainly, the patients very rarely want to give up.

We're curing very few diseases. With most diseases we are trying to either prolong the life or comfort the patient. Ok, I got this patient with lung cancer. Even if I can't cure him, I am able to give some quality of life, for a few more months or some cases a few years, that's just fine. That's rewarding you know. I just had an example of that two months back, less than two months back. It was a woman, about 35, with breast cancer. Lung metastasis, both lungs. She was intubated. She was conscious, fully alert. There were mets in the bones, there were mets in the liver, but it was the mets in the lungs which was about to kill her. I gave her another course of chemotherapy. A week later she was extubated. Two months later she is home and is doing quite well. She's doing her household work. She does get tired, but she's still quite ok. Her chest X-ray is showing quite a bit of improvement. I know this is temporary and she knows the cancer is going to progress again. And a few months later maybe, um . . . we won't tell her anything more than we are able to.

But for that three, or four months she got, ok, that's my reward. That's my reward. I feel that's she's smiling and she's happy and that makes it just fine. Yes, the satisfaction that you get some quality of life for a few more months helps make the job more meaningful.

You have patients that if you cannot cure you could comfort their pain by giving proper pain medications. When everybody's going to die, who gets it? He died and this boy with the colon cancer and liver mets, he has been here for some time, doing well. He's going to die. Sometime with the next six months or a year, but look at it, you know, I can't give up on that. Yes, it does, I suppose. The younger patients do affect you more. But you know what affects me more is the family support of the patient. If there is a family involved with a given patient who is asking that person to live, to be out of the hospital, to get better, you forget what the age of the patient is. Yes, that happens, the family does not come around. But I find that to be the minority. I find the most involved person is the spouse. And many times after the patient has died, the spouse now has nothing to do. May be she was involved full time in his life, all these years, two years, three years, four years. And now all of a sudden things have changed. So, no I generally find that there is quite a bit of spousal involvement. Some cases the family, the children to a large extent, but spouse is the most involved with the patient. Usually there's somebody there to, well you know, care about them.

No, there is no physician support. They don't talk about the subject. They just don't talk about it too much. I, I find it a lot easier to talk with nurses about these things. I'm more apparently emotionally and philosophically involved with things now than I used to be when I was younger.

Probably bad, I would say. I think the reason it's bad, uh, as I told you I'm not so distant from the patients. Last night I was thinking about this patient, at 11 or 12 o'clock. I know I didn't do that before. I've been doing it much more in recent years than I used to. I guess that I'm getting too involved. I wouldn't say right now that I'm emotionally exhausted, but I do feel that I'm more emotional than I used to be.

I have changed. It's hard to confirm a time, but it's probably about the last five years or so. I don't think it would inhibit me in being a good doctor, but I know it can exhaust you. That would probably be the down side of it. One thing I can say is that I get more headaches nowadays. I keep a bottle of Advil in a drawer, which I never did before.

I'll tell you why. I'm more involved in the oncology cases because where we are giving more chemo the patients are living longer. When the patients die in a shorter period of time you have less involvement with them. But when the patient is responding they're living longer. You have a longer period of time involved with them, you know, so . . . Yeah, exactly, I hear what I'm saying. So the patient's are living longer, so you have more time with the patients. What was happening before was that we had less effective therapy. We would treat and then patients would die. Now we have patients who are in remission. So when they are in remission you're seeing a good time with them, you know. They are happy, you are happy with them, all right? Now when that patient lapses again you know that you have gone over a period of time that you had with the patient before.

> Mark: What you're saying to me, you came into this field to help people . . .
> Dr. Ahmed: Yeah
> Mark: Extend lives, just like you said . . .
> Dr. Ahmed: Yeah
> Mark: Improve their quality of life. And by the same token, while you're doing this, while you're getting this meaningful satisfaction, you mentioned that before . . .
> Dr. Ahmed: Uh-huh
> Mark: By the same token, it's hard for you to deal with.
> Dr. Ahmed: It's getting harder and harder to deal with.

How do I balance it? I think, when anyone dies, you know that's it. But yeah, they're living longer. I guess we could share other emotional aspects with our colleagues. But as I said, we, the physicians don't do that. I don't know. It could be I suppose that everybody feels that it's not so good to talk medicine. We talk chemo, we talk how busy it is, we talk about it, which is what it is, but this not the thing we talk about.

I suppose it would help if there were more support for physicians. I find it easier to go to the nurses. Very much so, very much so. Well, I think they are good listeners. Second I think they express their feelings. You can mutually express feelings to each other. So, I do find it comradely, a lot more comfortable with the nurses in talking. I just don't remember talking about the emotional aspects among the physicians. Yeah there is that emotional line you just don't cross.

The positives to these changes? Well, I guess it's positive that you can tell the next patient about the positive effect of your previous patient. I feel more confident as a doctor. I mean I feel that I'm more or less on solid ground. Partly with the knowledge that I've gained and partly because of all the experiences I had over the years. So you put together both of them and I can make a pretty certain diagnosis and feel more confident about the types of treatment.

There is still quite a taboo about cancer and I keep pointing out to the patients again, and again, that cancer doesn't necessarily mean the end. You know, you get cures in some situations, you get responsive prolongations, or substantial survival in other cases. You can do enough to comfort the patient for the period of time that the patient is going to live. I wouldn't say that there's glory here, but I think that it is very satisfying.

*   *   *

Dr. Ahmed impressed me with his down to earth manner and highly caring and sensitive outlook toward his work, colleagues, and patients. What is an integral part of this narrative is Dr. Ahmed's initial struggles, and eventual openness toward a changing medical world. Few people I spoke with have evolved as much professionally and personally as a result of working with terminally ill people.

Dr. Ahmed is still the director of hematology and oncology at the same city hospital in Brooklyn, New York where we first met ten years ago.

DR. GRAHAM

Am I enjoying medicine? That's a very tough question. That's a very open-ended question. I would prefer not to work. If I have to work I prefer to have something less stressful, but I don't think I would enjoy doing something that was inane. Yeah, I'm enjoying it. I would prefer to be home reading, having a family, I would much prefer that.

What do I find so stressful about this job? Are you asking about being a hematologist/oncologist or about being a physician, because they are two different things?

As a physician I don't have fixed hours. I'm on call all the time. My beeper goes off at two o'clock, four o'clock in the morning, two o'clock in the afternoon. I like being a doctor, it's very nice, and it's intellectually challenging. You get to take care of people. You get to do some things that are worthwhile and important. People are not very appreciative. At first that bothered me a lot. Some patients are, and I think cancer patients are more than most other patients, which is why I am an oncologist. But also people are very, very demanding, especially cancer patients. So, it's a double-edged sword, you get people who are grateful but they are also very, very demanding. Everything is very stressful about it, people are sick, their health is in your hands and that is difficult. And the time commitment is quite overwhelming, so, I don't know if I love it, I like it, it has it's definite benefits. I don't think there is anything else that I would want to do. This is just not an ideal one.

Since I started being a physician things have changed and become much more unpleasant than they were ten years ago for doctors. I've been practicing medicine here for a year and half and four years before. I worked here for four years before I went to _____, where I was a fellow and attending physician. I loved my fellowship. I didn't like my internship or residency any more than anyone else as far as the sleep pattern problems, but I loved my fellowship. I would have loved to stay a fellow forever. The fellowship did not prepare me for the business stuff. At _____ my income was so bad that I had to leave there because I couldn't afford to live in the city and work there comfortably. I mean, I'm not pleading poverty, I made some money, but very little, so I left and came here. They are treating me very well, and I'm not going to tell you how much I make here. It's a much fairer system here than at _____, but it's a big problem. The finances are very different for a lot of people who go into medicine because they want to make a lot of money, or ten years ago, but now you are scaring people away from medicine by making it so difficult to earn a living. It's just a living; it's not more.

You don't get paid very well. You talk to somebody my age opposed to somebody who is ten to fifteen years older than I am and they'll tell you they will never mention that, and they would keep their finances quiet. I could tell you that I'm not a government employee and yet the government regulates how much I can charge a patient, and that is a horrible thing. It encourages doctors to spend less time with each patient in order to see enough patients to cover their expenses and make some money. If you could charge by the time you spend with the patient instead of by the diagnosis then we could spend enough time with patients who would be willing to pay for the time, to make patients feel comfortable and not have them hustling in and out of the office. And I'm not a government employee and the government should not be telling me how much to charge.

It's not just DRGS, it's Medicare. It's not only hospitalization, it's out patients. But Medicare tells me that I can charge for my office visits $50.00, of which the patient gives me $10.00 and Medicare gives me $40.00. If the patient doesn't give me the ten, I'm left with forty. If I spend the usual amount of time I like to spend with a patient, which is at least twenty minutes so they can have time to ask me questions and I can do a physical exam, I lose money. If you think about it, how much rent, tax, secretarial support cost you are losing money. So that the idea is to see people every five to ten minutes so you can make some money. So that is very stressful.

I would have a socialized medicine system for those people who can't afford healthcare and make sure that every person in this country has healthcare. If you make more than x, you pay for your care, you pay for your car, you pay for everything else, pay for you medical care also. I hate asking people for money. I think that the people that can't afford healthcare should be provided with healthcare by me. On the other hand, I had a large practice at _____ and they all had incomes that exceeded anything I will ever see in my lifetime and they paid, $40, $10 really, for their office visit because the government said I couldn't charge more. So I would change the system a lot. I don't mean to focus on that being the biggest problem. It's not a big problem. It's a problem. It's not the biggest problem, at all.

Well I guess it's the biggest problem, but it's not that big a deal, ok. You can change that. It's doesn't make me not want to be a doctor. It just makes me angry at the system, but it's not that I don't want to be a doctor because of it.

I don't have any idea. I can't answer that question; I really have no idea. You know what you decide to do when you are twenty years old. I don't even remember what made me decide to be a doctor. I really don't know the answer to that question. I don't know if I really knew at the time, but I certainly don't remember really what motivated me. It was not because I wanted to help mankind. It was not because I had a passion, at all. I guess it was probably easy to be a doctor as opposed to having to go out and find a job and struggle. It was kind of like the next thing I was going to find, so I went to medical school. I ended up liking it a lot. I think I am a very good doctor, but it's not a passion.

Oh, I love my patients. That's what I get out of it. I learn a lot, it's intellectually stimulating, but that's not the important thing. The important thing is that you get to meet a lot of people and take care of them and help them, whether they know it or not. When I said most patients are ungrateful, I think that, um, that's not my patients as much. That's why I went into oncology. I think cancer patients in general are very grateful for anything that you do for them, and in a different way than a lot of other patients who I saw when I was in training, which is why I went into oncology.

You know that is not a 100 percent true. The nurses are dealing most of the time with terminally ill patients. But we see a lot of people in the outpatient setting who are not terminal. It's the hospitalized people who are generally the terminally ill. We see breast cancer patients, 75 percent of them have been cured by their treatments. We see melanoma patients where 50 percent have been cured. So it's not the same thing in the outpatient setting, as it is in the hospital setting where the nurses are generally seeing dying patients all the time. The other thing is that I'm a hematologist also, so for every non-curable cancer patient I see, I see an iron-deficiency anemia patient who gets better and goes away. I wouldn't want to work as a hospice doctor. So it is a little different. The nurses here have it tough because they only see the sick people who require hospitalization.

You can help everybody, you don't cure people, but you can help them. One of the things that I think I do that a lot of that other oncologists can't do is say "Look, you're dying, we can't do that much here, we can make you feel better, why don't you go on vacation?" Most oncologists won't do that. I don't know, ask them. Ask them why when they have a terminally ill patient who's got a statistical chance of 1 percent of responding to chemotherapy, and you give them a round of chemo, and they don't get any better, why don't you stop and send them to Florida? Most of them don't, or at least when I was a resident and a fellow what I saw was people continuing to push the hell out of dying patients and I think that is cruel. Now, you know a small percentage of people that I do that to think I'm a horrible doctor because I don't have anything for them. But I think I'm doing them a service, and if they want to find a doctor who will poison them with chemo and they can throw up for the last few months of life, let them find that doctor. I mean, I like dying patients in a funny way because you kind of know where you stand, and you know what your goals are, and you don't have hopes that you are going to change an outcome, and unreasonable expectations. Instead you have this ability to make their life better for them in whatever way you can. It's not like with these chronic dialysis patients or these COPDS people who have to be ventilated and then unventilated. Those people drive me nuts. I would never want to treat people like that. I like people who know what is going to happen to them.

I'm also very straight with them so they don't have false expectations. I don't think it is cruel to tell people that they have a terminal illness. I think it is cruel not to because if they sense something is wrong, and they know something is going wrong, everyone imagines the worst anyway. So you are better off telling them straight because then they trust you in the future to tell them what is going on.

But I don't think the majority of the doctors do this. It's not malicious in any way. I don't really see how other doctors work very closely, so it's hard for me to know about communication gaps between the patient, doctor, the nurse and family. Nurses see it much more. Let's use a specific. If I have a patient who comes into the hospital with an unknown diagnosis and I find out they have metastatic breast cancer. The nurse is informed of the diagnosis so she knows how to deal with patient. The patient is informed of the diagnosis with the family present if possible. The patient doesn't get excluded unless there is something wrong going on. If there is something wrong with the patient's mind or emotional status then that's a different story. But a normal human being who doesn't have any pre-existing mental illness you don't walk into a room and say, "Hello, I'm the doctor and you have cancer and you're gonna die." I'm not sure I know what you mean by communication.

> Mark: I've spoken to nurses and I've spoken with physicians. Nurses tell me sometimes that doctors don't know how to deal with this. If someone has a terminal illness you won't see the doctor on the floor for three weeks, they just avoid it.

You're using the wrong word. If someone is pre-morbid and about to die, the doctor tends to step back from the patient. I don't think I do it, although I probably do it also because at that point you have absolutely nothing to offer the patient, so your role is limited. It's, it's disturbing to constantly walk into a room and not be able to do anything. What I am saying is that giving chemo is not the only thing you do. By going into the room and holding the patient's hand for five minutes and saying, "Don't worry, you won't be in pain, don't worry you're family is okay, don't worry, whatever," you're helping the patient, but these are really things that a nurse can do, a doctor doesn't have to do that. I do it because you've established, um, ten months of rapport with a patient or five years of rapport with a patient, and you don't desert them in the last three weeks of their lives. But, for example, I have been called in to see a patient who's being taken care of by doctor x, the patient comes with lung cancer metastasizing into every part of the body, and I haven't talked to the patient. I don't know this patient. I've never met this patient. The patient doesn't need me. They have doctor x, and I go to Dr. x, and I say "the patient has lung cancer all over his body. There is no good chemo; there is nothing we can do. Send him to radiation, get him tallying. I will follow along with you, but he's your patient, and I'm not going to do very much. I won't get emotionally involved in the last three weeks of this guy's life. But if you're the doctor, your not just a chemo-therapist, then it takes a different role. Doctor x is the primary care provider and if I have to be a consultant, I'm not going to go in the room in the last three weeks and hold the patient's hand. It's not even something the patient would want. Who wants this stranger to tell me I'm dying?

I think the nurses do see that a lot and I think a lot of doctors do escape from the patient's lives at the last minute. I tend to sometimes, more because the patient's sleeping or out of it and there's nothing I can do, and I'm in a hurry, uh, but I don't think I do because patients are looking for me to be there. Maybe I do. Fortunately the nurses on the floor will say, "Look _____, you haven't been in the room, and she's looking pretty crummy. Why don't you go in and say hello." I mean I got that about a patient in hospice yesterday and I went down. But, I think doctors get scared. I think everybody gets a little scared. No I don't do that at all, think about my mortality.

A lot of the cases, the more I think about it, there's not that much you can offer the patient, and you have ten other places to be and people to see. You're less likely to go into that room unless they're looking for you to be there. If they're looking for you to be there, then that's fine, but I mean I do try to go in every day and see if the patient is comatose. If so I may turn my fellow in instead.

It bothers me, it's sad. It's just more. You know, I'm thinking, I lost a patient a few months ago who's just a lovely lady. Who I've been taking care of for about three years, and I stopped going in because she didn't know whether I was there or not, and I had one million other places to go. She really should have been in a hospice, but she was rejected from hospice because of her insurance. So I just, you know, walked by the room, wave, she didn't know if I was there or not. But, what does matter is if someone's looking for you to be there and to help and you're not there.

Most of my patients I don't have a wonderful friendship, or rapport with. But I think I get to know them. If you're a good doctor and you're thorough, you get to know your patient pretty well because you have to ask certain questions and you just get to know them very well. But, uh, there are only a few patients where I've had an emotional, awful time of dealing with their death. You can't do that. It's not fair to them. It's not nice to them. They don't want you to be that emotionally involved with their care. They want you to be intellectually involved with their care and they don't want you to fall apart for them because they have to fall apart, and they need someone that's not going to fall apart. And you know, there are nurses who say, "Oh, it's so wonderful to cry with your patients." Well, I think that's bad for the patient. Oh yeah, I have certain patients, I mean, I had one patient who I was like, you know, we'd sit in a room together and pass the Kleenex back and forth, and I was fine, but I don't think that's really good. Because your doctor is not supposed to be crying with you, they're supposed to be strong for you. And it's one thing to say things to patients with compassion and make sure the patient knows that you feel for them and that you're involved with what's happening with them. It's not anything to crying; you're not helping them by doing that. I don't think. I don't think it's that wonderful to see a doctor cry. I happen to be one of those doctors that cry, but I don't think it's great. I think it's one of my least virtuous qualities about being a physician. Absolutely, without a doubt. Without a doubt.

Yeah, I guess I was more emotionally attached to my patients when I first started as a physician, it's also the type of patients. The persons I get attached to are my age. No, it's not the mortality issue. No, there are people if I had met them at a cocktail party I would have been friends with. So I can't help it. I can't not like them just because I'm the doctor, so it's a little bit different.

Mark: But you felt you were more attached earlier than you are now?

No, to tell you the truth, I think it's more, it may be, I mean I can't really tell for sure, but I think it was more that there was a certain number of patients who were my age who I could have chit-chatted on the phone with, you know, and be friends with and gone out to dinner with. Those are the people you tend to; at least I tended to befriend. In a funny way it's more emotionally draining. That's when I related to them because I don't do that for that reason. It's not that I force myself not to, but I don't tend to say "Oh, that could me." That doesn't enter into it.

Minimal, yes, but minimal. I think it's not a wall really. It's just looking at things in a certain professional way so that you're doing the best for the patient. You know it's easy to cry in front of a patient if you think it's going to help them, but it's stupid for the nurses who say to me "Oh, you should cry in front of your patient." I think they're stupid. I don't think it has anything to do with it. It's being very, very superficial and silly, too me. I wouldn't want my doctor to cry. No, no, no, it's not being stoic. Crying doesn't help anything. I mean, you know, obviously when I tell somebody they have cancer I don't stand there with a stony face. I don't smile at them, but I don't cry too, I think it's pointless.

You go back to the nurses that tell you doctors should cry in front of their patients or whatever, that's not what they're really saying, at all. They're saying that the doctors should treat the patient like a human being. It's not the crying.

Mark: But, to them that's part of being a human being, that's all.

But that's stupid because I always treat my patients like human beings, and I try not to cry. And I think that ___ treats his patients like human beings and I'm positive ___ never cried in front of a patient, well maybe once. But, you know that's not the point. You treat the patients like you would want your mother to be treated.

Yes, I do believe there should be some emotional psychological support. For the nurses, oh forget the doctors, doctors are a totally different thing. I'm talking about the full time people who are chronically in this environment, because doctors are different. They're out, they're in, and they're doing a million other things. The nurses, these nurses on _____ all they do all daylong is take care of these patients. But I think there is a lack of cultural uniformity, which would make a support group very difficult.

You know it's hard to know whether they just have had in their nursing training a way to put up this wall, but they seem to have a wall. And also these people float in and out. Our floor is not staffed real well right now because we lost the head nurse. So it's really not a good time. But generally yes, I think they should have support sessions. I don't even know if they need a psychiatrist or psychologist. I think what they need is somebody sitting there and saying, "Did you see what happened to Mrs. Smith today? Did you see what Dr. X did?" with impunity. It worked pretty well at Columbia where they just kind of had their own impromptu sessions, but they don't have that here.

I don't think doctors talk about these issues and I don't think they need to. I think people should talk about their feelings and all that kind of stuff, but I think there's a big limit to how much people should talk about their feelings. If something is bothering me, I talk with _____ about it for five minutes. I feel better, you know. I don't need a support group. I wouldn't go into a support group. I'm not sure how much of a need there is. I think there is much more of a need among nurses, you know people who are just chronically sitting on this floor, watching people dying and wiping their butts. It's very different. Nursing is very tough. It's a very tough field to be in different than hospice because up there you're trying to make people better. In hospice, it's kind of nice, you have absolutely no expectations and you just gear yourself toward making the patient comfortable. That's really wonderful nursing in a funny way. No, not like helping them die, they'll die on their own. I mean, it's just making them feel better.

I am optimistic about the direction the cancer environment is going in. I think you're going to see, you know, don't ever put so much pressure on us, so much emphasis on the humanistic side that you forget the more important side is the intellectual side. What I mean by the intellectual side is, well, first of all, research is very important, but I am talking about when you're talking about a doctor. I would rather have a really smart doctor who is a jerk, than a dumb doctor who is very nice. Yeah, someone who's going to provide good medical care. That should not be less important than somebody who is nice, caring and feeling and all that stuff. That's stupid compared to the fact that you want someone who is going to give you appropriate medical care.

I think that oncology 10, 20 years ago was very easy to practice. More of it was "Oh, poor honey" patting on the back and holding hands. Today you better be very smart and know what's going on. Try new things and push your patients a little bit because you can do something good for your patient's health. And that should never be overshadowed by whether you're nice. I try to explain that to my patients. They don't like Dr. X and it's like he's the smartest person around, go to Dr. X— if you want someone to hold your hand, go to your sister, go to your husband.

No, there are no myths surrounding the expectations of cancer care. If you take care of people the right way then they know what to expect. If you're honest with them then they don't have unreasonable expectations. Some do anyway, but that's what I was saying, that cancer patients have much less of unreasonable expectations than like a cardiac cripple. A cardiac cripple once in a while you can't make their heart better, you can't. It's funny, if you tell someone they have cancer they don't have the same unreasonable expectations.

I'll tell you something. I think teaching somebody about these things are a little bit silly. I think it is a lot experiential. And I also think that there are certain people who go through residency untouched by what they have seen, emotionally. And maybe they are lucky, but they are probably just the ones that go into gastroenterology. You kind of pick your field. Nobody who is emotion free goes into oncology. No one who doesn't care about being more than just a technical physician goes into oncology. Now, occasionally you're going to come across somebody who really doesn't belong in the field. But, I think basically people do fit their field.

*   *   *

Dr. Graham's dedication and thoroughness as an oncologist is evident. Her straightforward comments about why she became an oncology doctor, coping during stressful conditions, ways of communicating with patients and scientific care versus humanistic care for patients are core themes in this narrative.

Dr. Graham continues to be a successful oncologist for the hospital where we originally met.

A Symbolic Interactionist Look at Death and Dying

A perspective is an angle on reality, a place where the individual stands as he or she looks at and tries to understand reality. An angle will always limit what one sees, since other angles—many of which may also be accurate—cannot be considered at the time.

Joel Charon

OVERVIEW OF SYMBOLIC INTERACTIONISM

The narratives in Section One deal with a rare inside view of the human side of the medical oncology environment. Hopefully, these recorded death-related experiences from oncology healthcare professionals have provided readers with some purposeful meaning to their work and lives. My focus in Section Two is to respectively expand upon the reader's personal perspective of these stories by closely examining three death-related experiences taken from varied narratives within the theoretical framework of symbolic interactionism. I call the three death related experiences *Acts of the Self, Acts of Coping,* and *Acts of Communication.* Integrating three death-related experiences of oncology healthcare professionals with a symbolic interactionist perspective gives readers a chance to reflect on their own experiences in a more practical and theoretical manner. Once this insight is made readers can determine to completely apply, reject, or modify the narrative's and/or theory's premise for their day-to-day use.

According to Charmaz (1980), symbolic interactionism is "a theoretical perspective in sociology that assumes society, reality, and selves are *socially created* through interaction processes" (p. 17). Interaction processes, as the title suggests, is a symbolic one. Charon (1998) defines a symbol as, ". . . a social object, which is any object in a situation that an actor uses in that situation that has arisen socially and is understood and can be applied to a variety of situations" (p. 44).

In order for symbols to be accurately defined or understood, individual meaning must first be attached to them, and then mutually shared with others. Blumer (1969) states that:

> . . . human beings act toward things on the basis of the meaning that the things have for them. Such things include everything that the human being may note . . . These meanings are handled in and modified through an interpretive process used by the person dealing with the things he encounters (p. 2).

Fife (1994) adds that:

> . . . the symbolic interactionist perspective of meaning is predicated on individuals' specific cognitive response to particular events. Subsequently, behavior is based on these meanings which emerge from within the context of social life and are modified and dealt with through an interpretative process that occurs as persons respond to the circumstances that are part of their daily lives (p. 309).

The symbolic interactionist perspective therefore puts the study—and meaning—of human behavior squarely in the context of daily events taking place at the moment. Within these everyday moments, the meaning of human action results from multiple interpretive and reflective acts of reality constructed by people. This active and fluid image of human behavior is in contrast to conventional views of psychology and sociology that often focus on pre-established intrinsic or external social forces as determining causes of behavior people have no control over. As Blumer (1969) points out:

> . . . the process of human activity is not caught by ascribing action to some kind of factor (for example, motives, need dispositions, role requirements, social expectations, or social rules) that is thought to initiate the action and propel it to its conclusion; such a factor, or some expression of it, is a matter the human actor takes into account in mapping his line of action. The initiating factor does not embrace or explain how it and other matters are taken into account in the situation that calls for action (p. 16).

Judging from these opening comments, symbolic interactionism would claim that who we are, what we feel, and how we see the world is structured as a result of interactive processes between people. Resolving or explaining this interactive process does not begin in the mind (i.e., attitudes) or in orderly social rules of living (i.e., role expectations, or status positions). If one pauses for a moment, it becomes clear that one's life is not just an expression of pre-established feelings or societal norms that regulate behavior. Life is not that neat. Everyday new situations develop that are cause for concern where current rules simply do not work. Individuals then choose, however expansive or limited that choice may be, to socially construct, for better or worse, their reality through mutually shared symbols that are meaningful and verbally expressed. Although intrinsic and external elements are important they become important only in *helping* people define situation to situation. The meaning of behavioral acts, from a symbolic interactionist view, therefore, do not emerge automatically as by-products of psychological or sociological factors, but rather as creative products of ongoing human action. And, since individuals have diverse realities or perspectives, it becomes critical to get inside the defining process of human action in order to understand experiences people live through, such as oncology healthcare professionals who treat terminally ill patients.

In the area of death and dying, Charmaz (1980) claims that:

> . . . the symbolic interactionist perspective informs us that our conceptions of death, our images of the social world where death takes place, as well as the everyday actions that constitute the process of "dying," are socially constructed. Although death is a biological fact, what it means to us results from our socially shaped ideas and assumptions. In short, from this perspective we can only understand 'death' in the context of the definitions and assumptions we have attributed to it (p. 17).

Thus, from a symbolic interactionist perspective, the source of meaning inside the medical oncology death-related experiences with terminal patients can be found in the interpretive reality doctors, nurses, and social workers attach to them.

In Section Two our discussion focuses on how symbolic interactionism helps explain the interpretive reality oncology healthcare professionals attach to working with terminal patients within the context of three death-related experiences: *Acts of the Self, Acts of Coping,* and *Acts of Communication.*

CHAPTER 4
Acts of the Self

My aim in *Acts of the Self* is to provide readers with a symbolic interactionist perspective on the meaning of "the self" in order to gain deeper insights into the complex actions oncology medical professional's take while coping, caring, and communicating with dying patients. To accomplish this goal we will look at two aspects of the self entitled *Reflection* and *Identity Formation*.

REFLECTION

In the preceding overview on symbolic interactionism it was emphasized how people come to see their daily lives through social interaction. The meaning inside this interactive process was defined by understanding the unique, interpretive reality individuals attach to them and share with others. Consistent with this position was that reality and perspectives often are different from individual to individual, situation to situation, thus setting varied meaning of human behavior in the center of *action* between people. Since it is the person that cognitively dictates what is symbolically meaningful in accordance with specific situations, she or he has the "reflective" ability to determine what is and what is not important before, during, and after each event.

The process of reflection is an important tenant in symbolic interactionism. Charmaz (1980) notes:

> Since symbolic interactionist position is predicated upon the premise of defining interactive processes, it follows that the interactionist viewpoint heavily stresses the human capacity for reflection. This stress on reflection suggests an image of human nature that views human beings as reflective, creative and active (p. 18).

The significant aspect of reflexive processing is that it is an integral act of the self, which is a major area of interest for symbolic interactionists. Blumer (1969) underscores the relationship between the self and reflexive thinking when he says that:

> The possession of self converts the human being into a special kind of actor, transforms his relation to the world, and gives him a unique character . . . The human being may perceive himself, having conceptions of himself, communicate with himself, and act towards himself. As these types of behavior imply, the human being may become the object of his own action. This gives him the means of interacting with himself-addressing himself, responding to his address, and addressing himself anew . . . this reflexive process takes the form of the person indications to himself, that is to say, noting things and determining their significance for his line of action. To indicate something is to stand over it instead of automatically responding to it. In the face of something which one indicates, one can withhold action toward it, inspect it, judge it, ascertain its meaning, determine its possibilities, and directs one's action with regard to it. With the mechanism of self-interaction the human being ceases to be a responding organism whose behavior is a product of what plays upon him from the outside, the inside or both. Instead, he acts toward his world, interpreting it by what confronts him and organizing his action on the basis of the interpretation (pp. 62-63).

Looking over Blumer's words, we can see the symbolic interactionist view of "the self" as a social object controlled by the individual arising in interaction with others. Reflective thinking therefore is not a meditative or unconscious thought process. Rather it is a highly conscious self-dialogue with oneself regarding how he or she sees themselves in relationship with others and their immediate environment. Think of how often we talk to ourselves about things that are going on around us, and how we act in our surroundings. For instance, as an individual (e.g., doctor) acts toward others (e.g., cancer patient) and others (e.g., cancer patient, family member, or nurse) act toward the individual (doctor), the individual (doctor) acts reflexively by acting toward him-self or her-self, judging and addressing what is going around him or her in order to direct action toward the interpretation of events (e.g., discuss diagnosis, increase dose of chemotherapy, or feeling helpless). At the same time, other participants in this interaction (e.g., cancer patient) are also performing reflexive acts of self and interpretive meaning in determining their course of action (e.g., refusing to take more chemo).

The symbolic interactionist perception of the self is thus social in origin and is not, in psychological terms, a solid core personality moving from one situation to another. Instead, the self is an emergent and creatively adaptive symbolic *object* used for different purposes because each social interaction requires varied interpretations of meaning. As different perspectives are mutually shared by individuals, new interpretive meaning of events define and redefine their inter-action leading to new goals and unique acts of self within an evolving environment.

Cindy, the social worker from Section One, poignantly captures the relationship between the self and reflexive behavior in her narrative as she speaks about how the years of interacting with terminal cancer patients has changed the meaning of her work, and, who she is as a person:

> . . . This has been sort of a humbling experience for me in terms of limitations about who I am and what my work is all about. I don't have any answers to this question. I don't have any ideas how people get through this experience. However they get through it, if they can talk about it fine, it they can't talk about it, that's also fine. If they're in denial, so be it. If they're open to it, so be it. So, I see my role very differently in terms of how I'm interacting with patients. I come to this work forever as a student. I have not experienced this kind of trauma in my life. I have not experienced this at all. I have healthy parents and grandparents who have lived long lives without any of these devastating illnesses. I have no idea what the impact would be, how I would react. I have no answers, no answers to this. What I realize about my work, the meaning of the work, has been defined in the process of supervising some graduate students in social work for two years now. These students are very concerned and preoccupied with what they are doing, what kind of work they are doing, and how to measure it. Are they helping people? Is change taking place? And feeling that nothing is happening. What I think now is that showing up is ninety percent of the work; the courage it takes to come and sit with people and let them talk is the gift. You see, allowing them the opportunity to talk is the gift. And that is where the work takes place because they don't have the opportunity to talk about it in their private lives.

Cindy's interactions with cancer patients transformed who she was as a person and healthcare professional. Early in her career, as it is implied above and throughout her original interview, Cindy approached terminal cancer patients by automatically assuming there was a socially or medically appropriate way of interacting with them. She seemed to believe that patients were looking for her to control things, to help them overcome their fears of death and dying with the hope their lives would return to normal.

Over time Cindy began to realize that she was not helping or changing her patients' lives in the way she thought it was supposed to happen. With this realization Cindy started to act differently toward her working world, defining it by what actually was confronting her and organizing her action based on experiential events with patients, rather then what was learned in medical school or elsewhere. With this reflective act Cindy begins to direct her line of action toward listening to the different perspectives, needs and wants of her patients. If denial was called for on the part of the patients, so be it. If they wanted to talk, so be it. Less talk was the gift Cindy gave to her patients. More talk became an obstacle for change and growth. Based on the social expectations or perceptions of what a social worker should do and be Cindy felt this was a humbling experience in limiting her professional role, responsibility, and identity in terms of caring for patients. These words indicate that Cindy's originally view of her role as a learned expert in the field who was taught to verbally offer knowledge, as well as compassion and empathy in helping her dying patients was slowly dissolving away. They also show she redefined and redirected the meaning of working with cancer patients, and passed this newfound experience to her graduate students who gave her job new satisfaction possibly because they positively reinforced her traditional professional identity as care-provider.

From a symbolic interactionist viewpoint Cindy's ability to listen, and adapt to each patient's authentic wishes by self-determining how to feel, help and communicate with cancer patients, demonstrated how she ceased being a responding organism whose behavior was a pre-established product of the mind or social convention. Acts of the self is not limited to Cindy's death-related experiences; they shape the lives of each healthcare professional interviewed.

For example, toward the end of our interview Dr. Ahmed reflects on how his relationships with cancer patients have changed him as a medical professional and person because they are now living longer due to more effective therapy than was available in the past:

> I'm more apparently emotionally and philosophically involved with things now than I used to be when I was younger. Probably bad I would say. I think its bad, uh, as I told you I'm not so distant from the patients. Last night I was thinking about this patient at twelve o'clock. I know I didn't do that before. I've been doing it much more in recent years than I used to. I guess I'm getting too involved. I

wouldn't say right now that I'm emotionally exhausted, but I do feel that I'm more emotional than I used to be. I have changed . . . I'll tell you why. I'm more involved in the oncology cases because where we are giving more chemo the patients are living longer. When the patient dies in a shorter period of time you have less involvement with them. But when a patient is responding they're living longer. You have a longer period of time involved with them, you know, so . . . yeah, exactly, I hear what I am saying . . . What was happening before was that we had less effective therapy. We would treat and then patients would die. Now we have patients who are in remission. So when they are in remission you're seeing a good time with them, you know. They are happy, you are happy with them, all right? Now when that patient lapses again you know that you have gone over a period of time that you had with the patient before . . . I suppose it would help if there were more support for physicians. I find it easier to go to the nurses . . . Well, I think they are good listeners. Second I think they express their feelings. You can mutually express feelings to each other. So, I do find it comradely a lot more comfortable with the nurses in talking. I just don't remember talking about the emotional aspects among the physicians. Yeah there is that emotional line you just don't cross. The positives to these changes? Well, I guess it's positive that you can tell the next patient about the positive effect of your previous patient. I feel more confident as a doctor. I mean, I feel that I'm more or less on solid ground. Partly with the knowledge that I've gained and partly because of all the experiences I have had over the years. So you put together both of them I can make a pretty certain diagnosis and feel more confident about the types of treatment.

Throughout this interview it was apparent too me Dr. Ahmed enjoyed being a doctor. Becoming a doctor was his childhood dream. Once a hematologist/oncologist Dr. Ahmed's goal was to improve the quality of life of cancer patients to the best of his ability, since there wasn't much hope for long-term survival in the early years of cancer care due to ineffective drugs. In Dr. Ahmed's view, in the early years of cancer care the doctor-patient relationship was conventional in that the doctor was the one who controlled discussions and treatment options. Such discussions and opinions were often done in dictatorial manner, brief and to the point. In turn, cancer patients asked few questions regarding their overall condition or care. Patients expressed a lot of faith in doctors. In all, there was little dialogue between doctor and patient. This was the environment Dr. Ahmed and his patients knew and felt most comfortable in. It was an environment that mirrored his acts of self and sense of self as a person and doctor—an authority figure and expert in the area of oncology treatment and care. Someone above reproach.

This relationship also allowed Dr. Ahmed to keep a safe, professional distance from his patients who would ultimately die in a short period of time. Such impersonal behavior was expected of doctors, especially those treating terminally ill patients.

Over 20 years later, Dr. Ahmed has become more interpersonally involved with sick people who are no longer in his eyes just patients. I would suspect Dr. Ahmed would now call certain cancer patients, to vary degree, his friends. Dr. Ahmed not only now shares in his patient's thankful remission and longevity, he also personally sees if or when they die. It is hard to witness the death of patient, more so with one you befriend. As a result of the transforming environment and social interactions, one sees Dr. Ahmed reflexive thinking in action as he creates new and related acts of the self, lines of action, and meaning regarding who he is as a medical doctor and human being. For example, Dr. Ahmed sees, as did Cindy, the once stable socially scripted care-provider/patient relationship being uprooted. As patients lived longer, Dr. Ahmed found himself sharing in the ebb and flow of their lives, where fixed treatment options and minimal communication with one another were no longer appropriate. Consequently, Dr. Ahmed chose a line of action that took on a deeper communicative and emotional component toward his work with terminally ill people, where such behavior of oncology doctors is often viewed as the domain of nurses and social workers. At first he says this was a bad thing because of emotional exhaustion from prolonged interactions with patients. Later he says his confidence as a doctor has grown because he can use past and present knowledge of medicine to provide an optimistic outlook for his patients. Assisting in the improved quality of life for patients can bring on a sense of self-worth as a doctor and person, but at what price? Being in touch with the humane side of medicine is something Dr. Ahmed was consciously starting to learn, at the possible price of losing professional control. Without a proper balance between personal involvement and professionalism there can be the risk of burnout. It makes sense then another line of action the doctor took was speaking about his experiences with nurses who he thought could better understand his new acts of the self, instead of other doctors who had difficulty talking about emotional aspects of death and dying. His colleagues don't cross this emotional line. The support the doctor received from the nurses positively reinforced his unique acts of self-expression, line of action, and subsequent development of as a person and medical professional in similar fashion the graduate students confirmed Cindy's meaning of self-hood and her role as healthcare professional.

It is within the daily dialectic relationship with terminal cancer patients that both Cindy's and Dr. Ahmed's acts of self and sense of self, are at once a socially constructing and constructed reality. As Charon (1998) aptly observes:

> As we interact with others and self, we develop our definitions of what is taking place in our situations, and we decide on how to act in that situation. The stimuli do not affect us directly, we do not respond to reality as it really is, but to reality as we define it (p. 27).

We see through the experiences of Cindy and Dr. Ahmed that acts of the self and sense of self is social in nature. The self-acts and image of both healthcare professionals are seen emerging in interaction and changing, or remaining stable, due to mutually shared interpretive meaning of events. One cannot overestimate the importance of other people in the defining, redefining, and overall development of the self. Our sense of self becomes one of perception; a product of the appraisals of others in a kind of mirror, reflecting back to us as Cooley (1968) would say a "looking-glass" self.

If one accepts the assumption reflexive behavior is social, and is the primary source of relational action with oneself and others, it is therefore important to be aware of how we perceive other people's realities and how they view our own interpretations of specific events. As Charon (1998) notes:

> Self-perception is no small matter. The self allows the human to look at his or her own action in a situation. The actor can understand the others in the situation and the influence they are trying to have on him or her. The actor can appraise his or her own actions as they unfold in the situation. We understand our situations in relation to ourselves . . . and we determine appropriate action (p. 81).

For participants then to understand each others self-acts they must first reflexively look back on themselves as a symbolic object in interactions; and second, self-determine, and decide how to use suitable self-acts as a purposeful line of action to fit particular events. The reflexive acts of the self, described by Cindy and Dr. Ahmed, can thus be seen as a microcosm of a broader relational environment they and peers interact within on a daily basis. There are, for instance, several inferred acts of the self by Cindy and Dr. Ahmed in the excerpts that helped create who they are, such as self-perception, and self-judgment, and by-products of these acts like motives, emotions and past experiences, not fully explained in this section. However, within the broader relational oncology environment the interplay between perception, judgment, and identity formation plays a prominent role in determining "appropriate action" taken by healthcare professionals in dealing with distinct death-related experiences that include coping and communicating with dying patients.

Before looking at specific experiences linking acts of the self with coping and communicative behavior in the next two chapters, it would first help to use this background to elucidate further the process connecting identity formation with self-perception and self-judgment.

IDENTITY FORMATION

In the section *Reflection* it was learned, from a symbolic interactionist viewpoint, the reflexive acts of self are at once an individual and mutually shared experience-taking event occurring in social interaction. From this reciprocal process of self-perception and evaluation, the idea of who we are also emerge. Fagermoen (1994) helps clarify this position in her study on professional identity formation in nursing:

> Symbolic interactionism holds that self-information is a reciprocal process taking place in social interaction between an individual and her/his social and cultural context. In this view, professional identity emerges through a process of self-information in which social interaction and self-reflection are basic processes (p. 435).

Schlenker (1986) cited by Gudykunst and Bradford (1994) adds this practical definition of identity:

> Identity, like any theory is both a structure, containing the organized contents of experience, and any active *process* that guides and regulates one's thoughts, feelings and actions . . . It influences how information is perceived, processed and recalled . . . It acts as a script to guide behavior . . . and it contains the standards against which one's behavior can be compared and evaluated (p. 230).

One key assumption we can infer from each author's comments is that identity formation is an ongoing socially active process that embodies, regulates, and shapes one's beliefs, history, feelings and motives. Or as Schlenker, (1986) succinctly phrases it: "identity is a person's theory of him or herself" (p. 230). This view of identity formation is illustrated in my interview with the registered oncology nurse Vicky. In the last two pages of our talk she vividly describes what it means to her to be a nurse:

> A nurse isn't what I do, it's what I am. It's who I am so I don't live my life as anything other than a nurse. A nurse wherever I go. Whatever I do because that's my personality profile. I'm a caregiver. I make

nice. I'm the one who wants to like quiet everything down. Put a Band-Aid on the booboo. That's what I do. . . . I can't imagine doing anything else. I never wanted to do anything else. When I was little girl, I wanted to be a nurse . . . It was really my life's aspiration, vocation. And it's been as wonderful for me personally as I would ever have expected it to be.

In another passage, oncology fellow Dr. Adam paints an eloquent picture of how he perceives himself as an oncologist:

Sometimes I fantasize about being Michael Jordan. He offers something I can never offer and what I can offer something he can never offer. I can never entertain the world like he does. I can never make the 35.9 million dollars he does. He has financial security, but I have an emotional sense of security. I know I can help people right now. And I know I can always help people. I know in the long term he's going to be who he is, he's going to be famous. He enlightens children; he gives them a shining light. Someone has to be, most of us, on the bottom doing the dirty work, and I guess that's what I am. I would love to make thirty-five million dollars a year. I'd love to make one million dollars a year in this field, be more comfortable and not have to work as much as I do. I'm very happy where I am. Again, this is something that through my teenage years I saw myself doing. I'm living out what I wanted to be. I feel very comfortable with that.

Looking over the above passages, emotions, motives, and past experiences become integral components that aid in each healthcare professional's meaningful construction of identity, or what Vicky aptly calls a "personality profile." It is also clear how self-perception (Vicky: "A nurse is not what I do, it's what I am") and self-judgment (Dr. Adam: comparisons with Michael Jordan; " Someone has to be, most of us, on the bottom doing the dirty work, and I guess that's what I am.") play a large role in building identity.

From a symbolic interactionist point of view the self, motives, emotions, and past experiences acted on by Vicky and Dr. Adams are not primary sources of action explained from within the individual. They are labels or definitions one creates to use in a line of action; and secondly to use as a frame of reference from which the effects of events can be interpreted from within social discourse or interaction. As Gergen (1985) pointedly declares:

The mind becomes a form of social myths. The self-concept is removed from the head and placed within the sphere of social discourse. In each case, then, what have been taken by one segment of

the profession or another as "facts about the nature of the psychological realm are suspended; each concept (emotion, motive, etc.)
is cut away from an ontological base and is made property of the
socius" (p. 11). And according to Charon (1998): "Emotions, motives,
past, . . . and self-all of these are social objects, shared in interaction,
used in situations by the actor to guide decision making and action"
(p. 147).

In viewing the examples above it is clear that the picture one
ascribes to his or her acts of the self is inextricably linked to identity
formation. Our self-perceptions or image therefore mirror the way one
views his or her world and place in it within the social context of space
and time. It is both a stable and adaptable process, being the basis of
continuity between the past and present that provides a reference point
in which to examine meanings in situations and, thus, influence what we
do in every interaction. Often, as Fife points out (1994), "it is these
perceptions that give a sense of coherence to life in the face of loss,
change and personal upheaval" (p. 309). With this thought in mind our
discussion turns to *Acts of Coping*.

CHAPTER 5
Acts of Coping

The chapter on *Identity Formation* demonstrated how symbolic inter-actionists are curious about the kinds of personalities and world view people have that influence action and make sense out of who they are in relation toward others and everyday environment. In this chapter talk centers on how one's identity and ideology shape and justify present and future acts of coping by healthcare professionals treating terminally ill patients. In order to appreciate this interplay it is important to note society's attitude toward death, and the structure of its death system in which coping mechanism can derive.

THE SOCIAL CONSTRUCTION OF DEATH

According to Corr (1997):

> No society is without some system for coping with the fundamental realities that death and dying present to human existence...One interesting aspect of every society is its views on death, the nature of its death system and the ways in which that system functions (p. 39).

For our purposes, an abridged reading of Berger and Luchmann's (1966) social construction view of death will be the catalyst and framework in which a general look at society's attitudes toward death and acts of coping by oncology healthcare professionals, such as avoidance, will be discussed. Consistent with views of symbolic interactionism, a social construction perspective on death, and nature of its death system, illustrates how the link between identity, ideology, and coping mechanisms are symbolically defined and acted upon within an oncology environment.

In their book *The Social Construction of Reality* (1966), Berger and Luchmann (1966) give this description of modern society's constructed death system:

The experience of death of others and subsequently by the anticipation of one's own death posits the marginal situation par excel-
lence for the individual. Death also posits the most terrifying threat
to the taken for granted realities of everyday life. The integration of
death within the paramount reality of social existence is therefore of
greatest importance for an institutional order. Legitimization of
death must carry out the essential task—they must enable the
individual to go on living in a society after the death of significant
others and to anticipate his own death, with the very least terror
sufficiently mitigated so as not to paralyze the continued performance of the routines of everyday life. Such legitimization then
provides the individual with a recipe for a "correct death." The
primacy of the social objectification's of everyday life can retain
its subjective plausibility only if it is constantly protected against
terror. To be anomic, therefore, means to be deprived of this shield
and to be exposed alone to the onslaught of nightmare. The symbolic universe shelters the individual from the ultimate terror by
bestowing ultimate legitimization upon the protective structure of
the institutional order (pp. 101-102).

Let's look closely at how this socially constructed death system
helps shape identities, attitudes and acts of coping among oncology
healthcare professionals.

The opening comments read:

The experience of the death of others, and subsequently by the
anticipation of one's death posit the marginal anticipation par excel-
lence for the individual. Death also posits the most terrifying threat
to the taken for granted realities of everyday life. The integration of
death within the paramount reality of social existence is therefore of
greatest importance for an institutional order.

It is suggested in these remarks that the prospect of dying is
the ultimate threat to society members' daily realities, routines and
well-being. In turn, a social order, in the form of fear and repression are
necessary attitudes to propagate in order for people to get through life
socially and professionally. Perhaps this is why even though death and
the dying process is a matter of concern for most members of society it is
often evaded and not discussed openly.

Within this general social outlook on death, healthcare professionals have taken on primary responsibilities in treating and attending
terminally ill patients, while the role of family care and support has
diminished. According to Buckman (1997):

Contemporary society is going through a phase of virtual denial of death. Such attitudes are probably cyclical, and we may now be seeing this denial phase beginning to fade. However, the price of the current attitude of denial or avoidance is paid by the person whose life is threatened and who has to face death, and by those who look after and support the patient-the family and the professionals (p. 142).

The practice of protecting an individual from the nightmare of death and dying possibly has its roots in family interactions with children after someone dies. Kübler-Ross (1969) has stated that " In a society where death is regarded as taboo, discussion of it is regarded as morbid and children are exclude with the presumption and pretext that it would be too much for them" (p. 7). Corr (1997) suggests:

many of us are now living in a "death-free generation" one that is born, lives through infancy, childhood and adolescence, enters into adulthood, marries and has children, all without experiencing the death of a significant close family relative. . . . If this is the pattern of their confrontations with death, perhaps it is not surprising that death seems to be a stranger or an alien figure which has no natural or appropriate place in their lives (p. 33).

Due to the unnatural or inappropriate place that death has in many people's daily lives, dying in modern society is more likely to take place outside the home of a family. Nuland (1993) observes that in

recent generations we have added something new to the method of modern dying. Modern dying takes place in the modern hospital, where it can be hidden, cleansed of its organic blight, and full packaged for modern burial. We can now deny the power not only of death but of nature itself (p. 15).

As a result, care for the terminally ill has increasingly involved the work of healthcare professionals and affiliated hospitals. In addition, the family member roles and responsibilities have been greatly diminished in supporting a dying person at home, as terminal patient's care becomes the exclusive business of specialty healthcare professionals and institutions. Buchman (1997) states: ". . . As the extended family has disappeared so dying has become the providence of the healthcare professional and or institution: most people have lost that sense of continuity and now regard the process of dying as intrinsically alien and divorced from the business of living" (p. 142).

The middle passage (Berger & Luckmann) points toward the functions of society's constructed death system:

> Legitimization of death must carry out the essential task—they must enable the individual to go on living in society after the death of significant others and to anticipate his own death, with at the very least terror sufficiently mitigated as not to paralyze the continued performance of everyday life. Such legitimization then provides the individual with a recipe for a "correct death."

A key function of a social death system is to allow people to effectively perform common roles and tasks in the present and future following the loss of significant others. Maintaining control and a sense of balance are critical acts of coping when confronted with the death of others and one's mortality. As the paragraph suggests, while the individual engages in the coping process the meaning individuals arrive at during the death-related experience is meant to provide coherence, not devastation to one's self or world view.

Similar behavior is seen in the oncology environment.

Fife (1994) observes that "within the context of a highly threatening event, such as serious illness, the process of defining meaning involves efforts to understand and put in perspective the occurrence of the event, and to comprehend it significance for one's self and one's future life" (p. 311). Marcy, the hospice nurse, and Dan the oncology nurse, talk about the struggles in coping each day treating dying patients; what it means to be a nurse; and how caring for dying patients helps put their future and own mortality in perspective.

Marcy:

> One of the things I can give to people is a sort of living testament that it's possible to survive, and survive fairly well. In spite of being a cynic, I still find the work that I do life affirming . . . The life-affirming thing about this is I think it's really a rehearsal for my own death. All this that I am doing is learning how to die in case of being caught unaware here, or on my way home, or whatever, so that I do it gracefully. I don't know if there is a balancer out there who's balancing all those wonderful things. These mitzvahs that I give, so when my turn comes, and I'm lying in some bed in Calcutta someone will come and lift me up and put me in this clean white deathbed that I fantasize about. As much as I'd like someone to be there, I just don't know if there will be. That's where the cynicism comes in. I hope that having done this so many times and having witnessed so many people in life and so on, that I will be able to do it for myself. I will not need anyone to do it for me. I will be able to do for me.

Dan:

> I worry about my own death and that nobody will be there for me. Supposedly if you give you get back. I don't know if that's necessarily true. One hopes that it is. One hopes that it's not all in vain what's one doing. I have a terrible fear of dying alone. I hope there will be somebody compassionate there to help me out. I don't care if it's a nurse, but I hope there will be some caregiver around me who is really nice. I mean, I make my patients feel good. . . . I've had people say to me, "How can you be around all those dying people?" It's actually quite easy if you get in touch with that in yourself, its very easy to take care of these people . . . This is very uncomfortable for some people to get in touch with that part of themselves. It's usually done very privately and it takes people a long time, if ever, to get in touch with that part of themselves, which could be your soul, I don't know. That's interesting, to talk about someone's soul, isn't it? Each death diminishes you, and this job takes a piece of your soul, everyday. And the soul is very hard to replace. That hurts; that hurts terribly.

We see the fine line Marcy and Dan are walking while putting their professional and personal lives into balance. Their comments are almost religious in context, as they believe that their compassionate efforts with terminal patients will hopefully reward them a similar graceful, or "correct death" when they die. Such comments also give insight into what motivates them to do this line of work. The deep meaning Marcy and Dan attach to their daily care of dying patients provide them with strong professional identities and worldviews, which are seen influencing their present acts of coping and future possibilities. In the end we see Marcy and Dan attempting to, as Fife (1994) says, ". . . put the event in a perspective that does not denigrate the self, that is not overwhelming, and that makes the situation seem manageable" (p. 311).

The third passage (Berger & Luckmann) states:

> The primacy of the social objectification's of everyday life can retain its subjective plausibility only if it constantly protected against terror. To be anomic, therefore, means to be deprived of this shield and to be exposed alone to the onslaught of nightmare.

These words reinforce the notion that in order for people to function effectively they must be socially shielded against the thought of dying. But it also adds that to be anomic, or different, from others means to be deprived or have no social barriers against the thought of dying; thus the individual is left alone exposed each day to the nightmare of facing the prospect of dying. Many readers can probably recall how vulnerable they felt after a significant person in their life died. Imagine what it must be like for the medical professional who faces loss and mortality issues everyday.

Novack and Suchmann (1997) have reported that:

> Experiences with death and fears of vulnerability and death pro-foundly influence physicians care of chronically ill and dying patients . . . Because of their attitudes and belief about death or emotional pain of losing a patient, physicians may become distant or over involved or may under treat or over treat the terminally ill (p. 505).

Citing Dr. Barnard (1994) Vachon (1997) speaks of the tension between the promise of intimacy and the fear of the health professional's undoing in the care of the terminally ill:

> We live in the tension between the promise of intimacy and the fear of our undoing . . . The fear that accompanies moments of intimacy in palliative care-free of entering intimately into another person's agony and the fear of being overwhelmed by suffering, chaos, and disintegration (p. 924).

The oncology environment is undoubtedly a stressful one for patients, families and healthcare professionals. Vachon (1997) notes:

> Not only do patients and their families suffer distress when con-fronting terminal illness, so do those who care for them. The profes-sional caregiver can experience stress in response to working with dying patients as well as in response to the death of a particular patient (p. 919).

In the following passage, Dr. Williams strikingly describes the constant vulnerability, tension and role stress endured in her relationship with certain cancer patients:

> You have somebody who just won't die, do you understand? The ones that have so much cancer, I don't know how he's walking. Do you understand? And this is true, you see people who have a lump on their neck, you give them radiation therapy. They develop another lump on their breast, so you give them more chemotherapy. This goes on and on and on. You always have this patient, always with a complaint, always with a problem.
>
> So the longer they live the more emotionally attached you become?

Of course, of course this happens. And to me it's very difficult in young people. This is difficult. I do a lot of breast cancer. And I have a lot of young women, 30-50, you know, that are active women, mother, sisters, wives, those kinds of things. And you see a little bit of their lives, you know, just slip by, you understand? You see something has changed, their sexuality changes, they don't feel as good as before, they don't care about themselves as much as before, maybe people around them are not as warm to them. Their relationships change. And you see it, and you see it, everybody becomes like a stranger, and you become more and more, I don't know what you want to call it; the friend, the priest, the social worker, the husband, the wife. You kind of fill some void for 15-20 minutes every two to three weeks or every three months. It drains you. It drains me. I see two patients like that in a week and I don't want to be on call, I just want to disappear. We do have people that seem to just stick to you and suck a little bit out of you. Because you are the doctor, you are here to cure me, to make me feel better, you understand? And you are not doing it. But why, what is the answer? It has nothing to with me. No, but you don't tell your patient that, but for me it is so. There is no answer to "What I do about it?" When it happens, it happens. Yes, there are periods of very high emotional stress, extreme. And it lasts a long time, a long time. You take it with you . . .

Concluding comments on a socially constructed death system (Berger & Luckmann, 1966) state:

> The symbolic universe shelters the individual from the ultimate terror by bestowing ultimate legitimization upon the protective structure of the institutional order (pp. 101-102).

In the overview section on symbolic interactionism, Charon defined the word "symbol" as any social object in a situation that a person uses in that situation that has arisen socially and is understood and can be applied to a variety of situations. The "symbolic universe" alluded to in the sentence can mean the use of any social object, i.e., reflexive behavior, the self, past, future, emotion, or environment which fits an appropriate line of action that guides behavior and helps explain the meaning and motivation behind varied, yet specific death-related experiences.

De Vries (1981), in his paper entitled "Birth and Death: Social Construction at the Poles of Existence," cites Sudnow (1967) in his ethnographic work on death in hospitals. Sudnow talks about

> ... death and dying as social states of affairs ... The notion of dying
> has a strictly circumscribed domain of proper use. The idea of dying
> appears to be a distinctly social one, for its central relevance is
> provided by the fact that it establishes a way of attending a person ...
> as a predictive characterization, it places a frame of interpretation
> around a person (p. 1047).

Sudnow's words can be used to further understand the behavior of
Marcy, Dan, and Dr. Williams in the following manner.

Marcy, Dan, and Dr. Williams use their symbolic world to bring
some coherence to a series of extraordinary events that can disrupt or
forever change an otherwise ordinary life. In this sense their acts of
coping inside a medical community coincide and perpetuate the beliefs of
a larger social death system that attempts to shield members from the
thought of dying, thus, legitimizing the protective illusion of
institutionalized order. For example, the personal and social perception
of what it is to be a nurse for Dan and Marcy—caring and compassionate
toward dying patients—are congruent. Dan and Marcy attend to their
patients in a way that mirrors both professional identities and belief
systems or world views. Consequently, their framing or interpreting of a
patient's dying process, as well as personal meaning behind their acts, is
usually expressed in positive spiritual and philosophical terms.
Dr. Williams' professional identity is closely tied to the social perception
that doctors save lives. Compassion and care for Dr. Williams and other
doctors, can therefore become an emotional burden that may effect
proper treatment and do damage to one's self-perception. Thus, patients
who cling and become attached can be an overwhelming experience for
Dr. Williams. Dr. Williams' attending of patients can then involve more
distancing or avoidance at certain stages of the disease than her oncology
counterparts. Additionally, the doctor's framing and interpretation of
individuals may appear more ambivalent or colder than how nurses or
social workers describe their experiences.

Erving Goffman's theory on the self and emotional management
may also offer additional insight into the social construction and
institutional order of death and the process of dying. Goffman's focus
on the individual's presentation of self attempts to "identify what
and whom is being presented, the ways in which roles are being played
and how both fit into the ongoing scene" (Charmaz, 1980, p. 29).
Goffman's perspective on the self is concerned with the construction
of action and its context, or what people *do*. Territory or social
arrangement of interaction is also important in determining human
behavior. Problems in interaction therefore become a conscious act

when there is disruption between individual action and sanctioned social or public behavior. Meanings and motives emerge when the participants start rationalizing and justifying their incongruous behavior, or as Goffman might say when "saving face," such as in the death-related experiences of Dan, Marcy, Dr. Williams, and other healthcare professionals.

For instance, it was conveyed at the end of Dr. Williams' passage that possible intimacy with her patients, and role expectation of saving lives, made her feel at times like she wanted to disappear. Avoidance or distancing is not an uncommon act of coping among medical professionals when treating patients as they reach the terminal stage of their disease. Such acts of coping and acknowledgment of one's limits can create self-judgments of helplessness, failure, and guilt for not performing as "publicly" expected; that is to save lives when interacting with patients who want and need more from their professional caregiver. Trying to live up to this public expectation and subsequent personal perception of what it is *to be doing* being a doctor often leads to varying degrees of stress, frustration, and too much or little treatment.

Seen another way, Goffman (1959a) claims that:

> A social establishment, *e.g., hospital/oncology unit,* is any place surrounded by fixed barriers to perception in which a particular kind of activity regularly takes place, *e.g., diagnosis, drug treatment, avoidance, stress, compassion, prejudice, moral judgements and disclosing of bad news* (p. 238). (emphasis added)

Goffman goes on to divide this regular social activity into three aspects of social reality-"personality-interaction-society" (p. 242). Within the three levels Goffman observes that a person's personality is developed through interactions with others in a society (e.g., nurse, social worker, doctor/patient relationship). In paraphrasing Goffman, it is when the person begins interacting with others, performance disruptions may occur that may alter orderly social norms and customs making participants awkward during conversations (e.g., Dr. Ahmed's close involvement with cancer patients who are living longer), shaming or discrediting an individual's social role or diminish a person's ego in his identification with a particular part (e.g., Cindy's diminished responsibility as a social worker; Dr. Williams not being able to cure her patients), or establishment and group (e.g., Dr. Ahmed unable to talk comfortably about his emotions with other doctors). These are consequences that disruptions have from the point of view of social structure.

The consequence of these disruptions is that,

> . . . we find that the self-conceptions around his personality, *e.g.,*
> *doctors save lives and must keep a professional distance from*
> *patients; Marcy and Dan's compassion toward their patients,* has
> been built may become discredited, *e.g., feelings of cynicism, help-*
> *lessness, guilt, frustration, and failure emerging out of violations of*
> *social morals and self-perceptions of expected behavior.* These are
> consequences that disruptions may have from the point of view
> of the individual personality. Performance disruptions then have
> consequences at three levels of abstraction: personality, interaction
> and social structure (p. 243). (emphasis added)

Looking over Goffman's words, the understanding of several
oncology medical professional's identities, motivations, competencies,
and emotions would be based on cyclical, socially constructed
interactions with patients bound by a medical setting that embodies
particular roles, customs, and values. Goffman's idea of presentation of
self is mostly concerned with the appearance of interactional
competence. As a result of performing within this medical environment
oncology healthcare professionals often engage in emotional
management of their appearance in order to live up to the social
expectations and obligations of being a nurse, social worker, or doctor.

Goffman sees emotional management as a form of "face-work,"
a term that could have fit into our discussion on identity formation.
Goffman (1959b):

> The term face may be defined as the positive social value a person
> effectively claims for himself by the line others assume he has taken
> during a particular event. Face is image of self delineation in terms
> of approved social attributes albeit an image that others may share,
> as when a person makes a good showing for this profession or
> religion by a making a good showing for himself (p. 5).

One can view Goffman's term "face-work" as a set of orderly, moral
actions taken to deal with events that offer actual or potential threats to
the positive social value a person claims for himself in course of some
social interaction. For many of us face-work or emotional management is
a part of our everyday life. Think of an airline steward and other people
working in public service occupations, such as teachers, cops, politicians,
or salespeople, who are expected to maintain a happy, smiling disposi-
tion because it is part of their professional identity. If anyone of them
lets outside or private factors disrupt their public routine resulting
in upsetting, misleading or harming others it can lead to ineffective

performance and embarrassment. Goffman thus sees most social settings divided into two parts: "one is public or 'front stage' behavior and two is 'backstage' behavior where most of us need a place where we can slip out of our roles and simply be whoever we want. The back region answers our need for privacy. By entering it, we escape the rigors of role enactment" (Trenholm & Jensen, 2000, p. 190). Seen from this perspective, when Dr. Williams mentions she wants to disappear, or can't tell her patients she can't find a cure, or Marcy talks about reciprocal care and compassion from others, these acts of coping can be seen as socially managed "face" saving strategies to maintain one's public perception of self and effectiveness as a healthcare professional.

With the help of Berger and Luckmann, other researchers, and personal life-experiences we have seen several ways in which oncology healthcare professionals attempt to control their interactions, environment, and themselves, while dealing with a daily onslaught of death-related situations few of us will ever encounter. At the same time, this talk has centered on the interrelated acts of coping and identity formation, while illustrating possible meanings and motives behind specific acts of coping by several oncology healthcare professionals.

Most significantly, these perspectives ultimately lead to an analysis of the meanings of human behavior derived from social interaction, which also include *Acts of Communication.*

CHAPTER 6

Acts of Communication

One recurring theme in the interviews was the way in which nurses, social workers, and doctors discussed how they communicate with patients and each other. This chapter will concentrate on the communication between the oncology healthcare professional and patient. Our talk revolves around two separate, though related acts of communication: *Disclosure* and *Metaphors and Euphemisms*.

As this talk takes shape it may appear these two communication acts would have fit nicely into the previous chapter on coping. I would not argue the point because everything we have spoken about so far can be embodied into "acts of communication." So overlap is naturally expected and welcomed. The reason for a separate heading, however, is to bring to the reader's attention how the meanings behind oncology healthcare professional's death-related experiences can be constructed from specific social acts of communication. Based on the communicative nature of this chapter, comments will also address the strengths and limitations of communication theories that propose the virtues of "effective" or "therapeutic" communication as a way of rationally explaining and handling death and the dying process.

DISCLOSURE

At the conclusion of the preceding chapter it was made clear that everything we have discussed essentially from a symbolic interactionist voice, arises from social interaction: symbols, reflexive behavior, the self, mind, emotions, perceptions, decisions, and acts of coping. More specifically we have seen how meaning or reality is socially interpreted and constructed among oncology healthcare professionals through their daily death-related experiences with cancer patients.

Since most social interaction is symbolic in nature, the acts or line of action taken by the nurses, doctors, and social workers communicate some type of meaning. In essence, symbolic interactionists see social interaction as never ending acts of meaning emerging from experiences. Since experiences and identities change over time individuals' response to specific situations vary in meaning. The varied interpretive realities are expressed and understood by the symbolic use of language. Fife (1994) states that:

> . . . within the theoretical framework of symbolic interactionism meaning refers to the nature of perceived relationships between the individual and his/her work that is developed within the context of specific events. Meaning exists within one's experience, it is understood in terms of one's responses to these experiences and it is expressed by symbols that constitute language . . ." (p. 309).

Marcy, the hospice nurse, talks of different interpretative realities between herself and patients being communicatively shared and understood:

> To establish trust I talk a lot with the patient. I tell them stories, true stories, of my experiences in life. I've been ill many times myself, gravely ill, so I have a personal story of experiences to draw on. Sometimes I make up stories, using metaphors from literature or poetry. I have a patient who is dying of cancer that has metastasized all over. We thought he would die over the weekend. I said good-bye; everyone was prepared . . . But he's suddenly going through some very exotic transformation . . . What struck me was that this man, who is 70 years old, a mechanical engineer who's always been staid is listening to rap music! He's lying in bed snapping his fingers to the beat of rap music. He's more interested in this form of music; he suddenly has a craving for it. This led us to a discussion of what might have prompted this sudden craving. Perhaps he was getting ready for his next reincarnation, I suggested. This is not a man who's into new-age stuff and I'm not either, usually, and if I were, he'd hardly be someone with whom I would discuss reincarnation, but it just sort of naturally flowed. We talked for about half an hour then he fell asleep, still listening to rap. I take what's happening in a patient's life at a given moment, in terms of what he or she is feeling and I try to use, as when we started talking boldly about rein-carnation. Sometimes I believe in it; sometime I don't. It depends on the time and place. I change too.

What stands out in this interaction is how Marcy places herself into the dying man's shoes. We see Marcy adjusting to a unique event by designing a line of action that places her into the role of her patient. The line of action places Marcy in a better position to understand this man's unique behavior. Evident by their thirty-minute conversation, the man would appear to have responded toward Marcy's experiences and interest by disclosing reasons for his actions. Symbolic interactionists' call understanding the perspective of another person "role taking." Role taking is an integral part of social interactions and corresponding acts of communication. Charon (1998) points out:

> Because interaction is symbolic, role taking is involved for both communicating and interpreting. Adjusting acts in relation to one another involves understanding the actions from the perspective of the other. We come to learn about the other and expect things from the other through role taking; the other in turn, comes to know us, what we are doing and what to expect from us (p. 155).

Taking the role of another person can also be an emotional experience, especially when the person can readily identify with the other individual. Susan Shott (1979), cited from Charon (1998), points out that role taking, "reminds us how often the emotions we feel are the result of taking the role of others in interaction: shame, guilt, embarrassment, pride, vanity, and empathy, for example" (p. 155). There are numerous remarks made in the interviews among oncology healthcare professionals that reinforce this emotional component of role taking. In the case with Marcy, we see levels of pride and empathy coming across as a result of her role taking. When permitted she takes pride in developing trust with her patients by disclosing her own life experiences or telling other related events from whatever source available. Additionally when appropriate she takes "what's happening in a patient's life at a given moment, in terms of what he or she is feeling . . ." to guide the conversation into a more meaningful relationship.

Marcy used a unique event where the potential for miscommunication, due to unexpected behavior, was very high as an opportunity to open dialogue in order to learn more about each other and what a dying man might be going through at the end of his life. It can be seen that the relationship between Marcy and her patient was constructed within particular joint acts of communication. Cited by Goldsmith and Baxter (1996) Duck and Pond (1989) observe:

> Our social and personal relationships are embodied or constituted by various kinds of jointly enacted communication episodes that occur. These episodes constitute relationships and the types of episodes partners enact together constitute a particular kind of relationship. Rather than viewing communication as something used by one relationship party to achieve his or her desired relational goals,

communication is conceived as an embodiment of a particular kind of relationship constructed jointly by the parties (p. 90).

Despite the mutually accepted role taking between Marcy and her patient it is likely that at some point ensuing disagreements will arise creating a communication impasse because of varied experiences and meanings people attach to them. As often as communicative impasses occur in our everyday relationships, they also appear frequently among oncology healthcare professionals and their patients. Surbone (1997) states that:

> In patient-doctor relationships many are the obstacles to communication. As in the rest of life, we face problems of language, reality and its limits, expectations and finally the presence of the incommunicable. Language is about words, about meanings, and about imagination. Language is the major obstacle to communication, insofar as it refers not only to linguistic property of a certain group of people, but also to the meaning that different persons attribute to the same words (p. 9).

The following passage from Dr. Richards, the oncology fellow, details the communication obstacles he faces with patients when disclosing bad news:

> With some patients there's a language problem which makes it difficult to fully explain their situation. There's also somewhat of a lack of sophistication so that you sometimes wonder if they have a good feel of what's really going on. You wonder what their concept is of their disease and if they understand their prognosis. It's hard to say if the information is not being understood or the patient just doesn't want to hear. If the patient speaks English well and is intelligent you have a better idea of what's denial and what's not being understood. I have a forty-year-old patient, a real nice lady who has a tumor. It hasn't gotten any smaller but it hasn't grown. It's sort of stable. I've been explaining to her that this is a good thing but she keeps trying to find out how much more chemotherapy she needs and when we're going to stop. She asks, "Why isn't the tumor going away?" I'm like, "Yeah, the tumor's not going away, but it's not growing. And where perfectly happy doing this." I've explained to her a lot that she's likely to die from this disease, but two years from now, not two months from now, as long as she's tolerating the chemotherapy reasonably well. This woman isn't like someone who has cancer. She dresses sharply. She's healthy looking. She's tolerating it fine. It's not even though it's hurting her quality of life significantly. So it's a little upsetting to me sometimes because I spend all this time explaining the situation to her and on her next

visit she'll ask me the same questions and we'll have the same discussion. She doesn't speak English perfectly well. She was born in China but I think she has a grasp of this thing. The bottom line is you're telling them bad news and they're looking for good news. It's as though they think if they keep asking the same questions maybe they'll get the answers they want, which is that we're stopping the therapy tomorrow. "It's all gone away and you don't need any more treatment." This hasn't happened though, and it's not going to happen.

On the surface this interaction between Dr. Richards and his patient would not raise too many eyebrows. Outwardly Dr. Richards is doing what he often does, tells a truthful diagnosis and recommends appropriate chemotherapy. In turn, the doctor expects the patient to accept the bad news and treatment with no difficulty, because he thinks she has a handle on this "thing"; is someone who doesn't look like she has cancer, nor has her quality of life suffered "significantly" from early rounds of chemo. Dr. Richards is following a customary social role of oncologist we saw earlier in Dr. Ahmed's earlier career as physician—remaining emotionally detached while providing professional care. His patient is also adhering to a social script of not wanting to die. She continually asks for good news when there isn't any, forcing Dr. Richards into the unsettling possibility of dealing not only with her anxieties and fears but his own as well, about death and dying. We also see expectations are not being meet by either party. Neither person is mutually role taking in order to use the communicative misunderstanding to learn more about each other's undisclosed concerns over disclosing end stage diagnosis and feelings of mortality, similar to Marcy and her patient. McCormick (1995) states that:

> barriers to satisfactory communication may arise from either the physician or the patient or both. The competent care of dying patients must extend beyond management of physical symptoms because patients may experience they're gravest suffering from fears and anxieties that is undressed in conversations. Conflicts arise when the disease progresses and the end of life approaches and the physician and patient have not reached agreement on their expectations (p. 236).

McCormick's words raise two important questions, "What is *satisfactory* communication?" and "What is *competent* care"? One can only base an answer from being in such a situation. Looking from the outside/in, however, perhaps *both* Dr. Richards and patient would like to privately talk about such concerns but they're "denial" is necessary in order to survive each day. Dr. Jones, oncology fellow, emphasizes the thought of non-disclosure or denial as a necessary act of communication and competent patient care:

> . . . When your patient gets sick and die, if you were to react like a family member or even a friend, you would be lost. So when problems come up and you're having a disagreement with another service or with other doctors about patient care and it's not going the way you want it to, you can't get all worked up about it. Because it will cause you to have peptic ulcers, or you'll have a stroke or you'll go crazy, or you'll just never be able to handle it. You'll have a breakdown, a nervous breakdown. We all have types of words, like desensitization and thought processes to separate the patient from ourselves, and their death process. I think desensitization is necessary because as I said, without it you would not be able to survive . . .

Jeff, the social worker, devotes a large part of his interview toward explaining the communication process between medical professional and patient. He describes favoring direct speech acts in telling patients about their terminal illness, but cautions us about the potential harm in words and disclosing bad news:

> . . . I'll try to steer them toward as much information as possible, because I feel they should know. Well, see, legally the doctor should tell. It is the patient's right to know, patients bill of rights is very clear about that. But, if a doctor or nurse—the doctor usually set the pace—the doctor usually doesn't have that good of comfort level with talking to people about terminal illness, or even prognosis or diagnosis of cancer, then you kind of have to go to the family. But, usually it is the family themselves who—the most frequent thing that I've heard is that if Uncle Joe knows he has terminal cancer it will kill him, which obviously is not logical. And they say it, and believe it when they say it. That knowledge itself, that hearing of words, will kill a patient. Oh yes, it's denial. I would say it is in at least a third, maybe half of my experiences . . .

Dr. Jones and Jeff's words underscore the point that choosing not to self-disclose information may be necessary to preserve the need to get through days professionally and socially by shielding oncology healthcare professionals—and patients—from the daily thought of dying. The comments made by Dr. Jones and Marcy also make us aware that acts of self-disclosure should not be forced. Self-disclosure is a personal choice, where individuals may divulge or not divulge information at any time during a relationship. Much will depend on the relational level and context between the parties. Yet, there is no guarantee that if one participant discloses information the other person will reciprocate. He or she may never talk about their personal experiences. Thus, too much information at one time can be overwhelming. One therefore should not assume disclosure of experiences is always effective or therapeutic; or that non-disclosure is always a negative act of communication. Looking at the passages from the perspective of a healthcare professional and patient makes it difficult to generalize from the outside what is satisfactory communication, or what is competent care and what is not.

What has been demonstrated is that acts of communication, such as role taking and disclosure, are a highly complex rule bound and unpredictable process in which oncology healthcare professionals—and patients—regularly manage and construct their meanings. In this sense, the role taking and joint acts of communication illustrated by Marcy, Drs. Richards and Jones fit neatly into both Goffman's "presentation of self"/"face-work" theory, and Berger and Luckmann's social death system, whose primary function is to protect society's members from daily thoughts of dying. We can, however, expand the way in which these communicative patterns and meanings between Marcy and Dr. Richards' patients are formulated by looking at Pearce's rule based theory on communication.

According to Pearce (1976) "An adequate explanation of interpersonal communication must account for the fact that people not only can but regularly manage their meanings." The process of coordinating and constructing these meanings "assumes that person's interact with others on the basis of perceived agreement or disagreement about what episode is being enacted and that these expectations are subject to confirmation or disconfirmation by the other person's subsequent acts" (p. 23). Marcy's passage depicts perceived agreement and confirmation with her patient to use their end of life discussion to open up further dialogue. Dr. Richards' experience would demonstrate the opposite.

In order to create the meaning of communication as episodic, Pearce divides communication exchange into three episodes. Episodes 1 consists of patterns of meaning and behaviors which are culturally sanctioned and which exist independently of any particular individual or dyad. An example of this would be the concept of a social death system. Episodes 2 consist of patterns of meaning and behaviors in the minds of individuals. These are private symbols that express individual's understanding of the forms of social interaction in which they are participating or in which they want to participate. From a symbolic interactionist stance, this episode involves reflexive thinking and interpretive realities or meaning that each participant attaches toward specific situations, which may or may not adhere to socially sanctioned modes of speech or behavior. To the extent that a person's episodes 2 resemble society's episodes 1, the person will be able to converse easily and be understood. To the extent that the Episodes 2 are idiosyncratic, the person will have greater coordination of meaning problems. Dr. Richards' interaction with his patient is an obvious example. But Marcy's is not. Symbolic interactionists might say Pearce's comments are pragmatically helpful in understanding the motives and meanings behind communicative interaction, but the drawback in linking episodes 1 with 2 in this manner is the assumption that communicative acts and general behavior is a neat and orderly set of events. They are not. Congruent behavior between people does not always mirror general social sanctions. They can be uniquely personal. For example, one might say Marcy's conversation with her dying patient also required greater management of meaning because their interaction contradicted social behavioral expectations. What is different about this interaction is that Marcy adapted to a unique set of episodes concerning her patient. In turn, she used the potential for miscommunication and misunderstanding of meaning as an opportunity to have her reality understood (i.e., her own belief system) while at the same time understanding what her patient was going through. The joint acts of communication between Marcy and patient created newfound interpretive realities and mutually agreed upon relational stability, irrespective of social linguistic or behavioral norms. Episodes 3 consist of the communicator's interpretation of the actual sequence of messages which they jointly produced" (p. 22).

Pearce goes on to talk about how "Episodes in which rules do not describe appropriate behaviors specifically or completely enough to guide actions or interpretations are designated as ambiguous" (p. 24). Concluding this line of thinking, Pearce comments on how

> . . . communicating with the terminally ill is an enigmatic episode. Partly because we institutionalized seriously ill patients, most people have not learned an Episode 1, which could guide them. Thrown into relying on their own ingenuity, these conversations are more troublesome and require more management of meaning than an enactment of a non-enigmatic episode (p. 24).

Again, Dr. Richards' passage is an illustration of this, but the reader may recall similar passages or situations appearing throughout many of the interviews or even in their own lives.

Pearce's view of communication is helpful in providing insight into how acts of communication help to construct, coordinate, and manage meanings inside the death-related experiences between oncology healthcare professionals and patients. Similar to Goffman in thought,

Pearce sees uncomplicated acts of communication occurring when social customs are publicly followed. Miscommunication or disruptions in communicative acts happen when approved linguistic and behavioral expectations are not meet in a particular context. As we have seen, the result of oncology healthcare professionals and dying patients misunderstanding each others messages and expectations can be the undisclosed fears and anxieties over an end stage diagnosis and feeling of mortality. We have also discussed that miscommunication or as Pearce says "ambiguous" episodes does not necessarily lead to a negative outcome. Ambiguous moments can led to open dialogue that may prove to be an enriching experience, as Marcy testified. By the same token, the implication that communicating undisclosed concerns over death and the dying process is preferred and will result in something beneficial is not always accurate.

J. D. Peters (1999), in *Speaking into the Air: A History of the Idea of Communication,* sheds some light into the historical origins of "therapeutic" and "effective" communication strategies. Peters does not directly connect his unconventional view of communication to the area of death and dying. His ideas though can perhaps be used in understanding more fully oncology healthcare professionals' and society's general communicative approach, misunderstandings, and impasses that take place during many death-related interactions with patients, family members, and peers.

According to Peters the chief impasses in contemporary experiences of communication can be found in the historic notion that communication, such as information exchange and therapeutic talk is both the cure and disease of public and personal everyday problems. Peters asserts since the days of Aristotle, thinkers such as Marx, Freud, Rogers, and Dewey, as well as popular cultural forms like drama, art, cinema, and literature have all grappled with and examined "the impossibility of communication between people" (p. 23). As a result, although the difficulty of human communication is historically and routinely evident, the term "communication" presently "evokes a utopia where nothing is misunderstood, hearts are open and expression is uninhibited" (p. 2). Peters critiques the interrelated notion of communication being historically identified with 'the mutual communion of souls" (p. 1), and communication breakdowns being persuasively thought of and studied as negative behavior. For Peters traditional notions and acts of communication often prove to rigid and do not resolve many intractable human troubles such as "language, finality and plurality" (p. 30). This is a profound thought that readers may identify with.

Think of a moment when you had difficulty finding the right words to say to a friend who suffered the death of a loved one. If you couldn't you're not alone, which would not surprise Peters. But if you did find what you perceived as the right words, did it make a difference in alleviating whatever feelings your friend experienced? Or perhaps when someone used comforting words to ease your pain from a personal loss, the intent was obviously a caring one, but did the words really ease any longtime pain from this experience?

As an example in the oncology world, recall Dr. Williams' comments in the chapter on coping describing her struggles coping and communicating with her patients. When asked if she had someone to talk to about her daily interactions with patients and responsibilities, Dr. Williams reply sounds as if she believes communication cannot solve life's finite problem of death or mortality:

> I have people I can talk about this with. Sometimes, you know, you talk about something like this, but it's no use talking about it, doesn't solve the problem, you know. Doesn't solve the problem.

Dr. Graham also talks about the limits of disclosure and therapeutic communication:

> . . . I don't think doctors talk about these issues, and I don't think they need to. I think people should talk about their feelings and all that kind of stuff, but I think there's a big limit to how much people should talk about their feelings. If something is bothering me, I talk with_____about it for five minutes. I feel better, you know? I don't need a support group. I wouldn't go to a support group. I'm not sure how much of need there is . . .

Perhaps there simply is no one formula "how to" communication approach oncology healthcare professionals and lay people can use when communicating with dying patients, love ones, family members and peers. As Peters (1999) observes:

> The achievements that technical and therapeutic talk usually ascribes to "communication"—understanding, cooperation, community, love-are genuine human goods. Even information exchange is indispensable, in its place. But the attainment of communicative goods can never be easy or formulaic so much depends on dumb luck, personality, place and time (p. 30).

From Peter's perspective, ideal communication or strategic discourse have good intentions in bringing logical, rational meaning to irrational behavior. It should be noted that there are worthwhile books in the area of death and dying that focus on using traditional, therapeutic communication models to aid healthcare professionals and lay people in dealing with death and dying (see Buckman, 1986; Van Servellen, 1997). The weakness, however, of ideal or step-by-step communication strategies used historically by academics and theorists is assuming human behavior is always or at the very least should be, orderly, static, and easily translated and explained. Often life is not that predictable where one can assume that perceived rational acts can help resolve irrational unexplainable behavior. For many people death, dying and intertwining communication processes equals irrational action that is ripe with misunderstandings. What's left then for Peters' is that miscommunication, rather than being cause for behavioral problems becomes an inherent and vital part of everyday life, where differences and diverse realities can be opportunities for learning and growth.

Symbolic interactionists see the individual as part of a social context, but also able to construct meanings in his or her environment mostly independent of pre-existing social and psychological conventions. Since people create, control and are responsible for their own actions the implication is that there can be no one single understanding of reality, or one single voice that can help define diverse experiences, as the death-related experiences from oncology healthcare professionals exemplify.

The researchers cited in this section, along with the experiential recollections of nurses, doctors, and social workers have helped in providing background into how communicative acts of disclosure help define and redefine participants interpretive realities and direct lines of action. Following we see in similar fashion how *Metaphors and Euphemisms* emerge out of social interaction to help shape relationships and meanings within the death-related experiences of oncology nurses, social workers, and doctors.

METAPHORS AND EUPHEMISMS

Metaphors and euphemisms are commonly used in lieu of direct expression or dialogue. Euphemisms are looked upon as a polite word or expression of a harsh reality like death and dying, while metaphors are the application of words or phrases to something it does not apply to literally, in order to set up a comparison with the literal usage. What is similar in both acts of communication is that they can be thought of as symbolic objects to help define and redefine the reality or meanings of varied death-related experiences.

In our culture the word "death" is often spoken about under an alias. Sexton (1996) astutely points out that the word "death" is rarely called by its own name: "The sheer number of metaphors we use in reference to human mortality is an index of our discomfort with the topic. In fact one would be hard pressed to find a type of reference to death in this culture which is frequently used and without metaphoric content. Rarely is death called by its own name" (p. 337).

Oncology healthcare professionals provide interesting, round about ways in which to talk about the subject. I meant to say talk about death. Take for example the following comments found in several interviews.

Dr. Richards, the oncology fellow, previously described his patient's overall knowledge of her terminal condition, as having a "grasp of this 'thing.'" The metaphor suggests that death may be considered an unknown, unapproachable, perhaps terrifying topic to outwardly discuss.

Jeff, the social worker talks of an individual in his support group metaphorically describing his diagnosis of cancer as a train, "you get on, a runaway train, where you don't know where the train is going to go, but you can't get off." The metaphor also implies that no matter what treatment is given, or how long remission is, the danger of cancer coming back will always be there for that person.

Dr. Jones, oncology fellow, paints this metaphoric picture of how each death of a patient builds up a defensive wall or way of coping: "I guess it's like how anyone becomes desensitized if you are hit with something long enough. Like if you have an allergy to something and they give that substance in small quantities repeatedly, so your body can build up a defense mechanism. It's the same thing with all these people dying. If you see it so much it lays another brick for the wall, on and on, so that they are actually helping you in a way, every patient that dies."

In another episode, Marcy, the hospice nurse, tells of a two-year-old child dying of acute leukemia, who metaphorically tells her, "I'm going on God's choo-choo train and I'm not coming back." The child died the next morning.

Reasons modern society and healthcare professionals use euphemisms involving death-related experiences is explored at length by Corr (1997):

> Prominent illustrations of ways in which death is forbidden in much of modern society include language of ordinary discourse, professional speech and communication about dying. It is important to pay attention to these linguistic practices because naming helps to define and to determine reality. How we speak says a good deal about who we are and the attitudes that we hold . . . (p. 36).

Dr. Williams, acknowledging her limits in saving lives, finds meaning in prolonging life for her patients in the most comfortable fashion possible. In turn, she perceives herself, along with her patient's perceptions, as the euphemistic "Angel of Death."

Marcy talks about her death in terms as a "clean white sheet" deathbed syndrome. Perhaps this euphemism is at once a reflection on how Marcy cares for her patients and that a pure, saintly death is something Marcy desires in return in the hereafter for her compassionate work with dying patients.

> ... when contacts with natural human death are more attenuated, language tends to objectify and trivialize death-related events. The result both discloses and contributes to a kind of distancing from important fundamental events of life itself ... (Corr, 1997, p. 36).

Dr. Jones reveals where certain euphemisms—and metaphors— among oncology healthcare professionals that lend itself to objectifying or rationalizing death originate:

> ... I think desensitization begins in the medical school, in the anatomy labs when you see the dead bodies. You know it's not human. It was human, but it's not someone you know, moving and doing things, eating and going to work. So you forget those human characteristics and use it as an object, to learn anatomy. And from there you go on.

> ... In modern society, euphemisms tend to shy away from honest and straightforward speech by covering death with linguistic shroud. People do not die "they pass away." Euphemisms of all sorts need not be condemned. Their weakness is in the unspoken assumption that direct speech cannot be sensitive and caring. Their danger arises when they tend to supplant direct speech entirely and when they themselves are emptied of content and become unfeeling cliches. Professional speech is euphemistic when it tell us that "we lost Mrs. Jones last night" or that she "expired." Perhaps the suggestion is that caregiver accustomed to think in metaphors of the conflict against illness see death as loss of failure in battle? More typically, they are simply unwilling to speak directly. Once entered upon this path, one easily ends up in bureaucratic hyperbole which redefines death as "negative patient care outcome" (Corr, 1997, p. 36).

Corr's insights, and the experiences shared by oncology healthcare professionals, make us knowledgeable of the critical link between language and acts of self and acts of coping. A symbolic interactionist sees the metaphors and euphemisms used by the doctor, nurse, social worker, and patient as symbolic objects helping define, or create this linkage, as well as guiding each participants decision making. Another way of looking at these particular acts of communication is that within the language and communicative act itself meanings and experiences emerge. Either way the acts take place inside a distinct social context.

Since symbolic interaction revolves around joint negotiation of interpretive realities, parties usually express the understanding of these meanings through verbal communication. Because of different world views and beliefs the coordination of understanding and meaning can be a smooth, muddled, or highly troublesome process. This social interaction makes words that construct metaphors and euphemisms vital acts of communication in which experiences and relationships are formed. In short, the perception of metaphors and euphemisms as a negative act of communication that shields healthcare professionals and patients from the prospect of dying may not tell the whole story.

For instance, Corr points out the possible negative effects of euphemistic and metaphoric usage in death-related experiences. In this case, certain phrases and expressions are communicative forms of strategic discourse to shield one's acts and thoughts from embracing mortality and the dying process in place of direct language or information exchange. The point being that direct use of language to describe death and dying is a better way of communicating and will make caregivers more involved, sensitive, and compassionate in their treatment, care and life. Perhaps, but doesn't it depend on one's perspective, as we saw in our discussion on disclosure? Why can't frequent use of metaphors and euphemisms also be considered a sensitive and compassionate form of communication and care?

Corr provides us with important and useful knowledge into how people use metaphors and euphemisms to avoid direct disclosure about issues surrounding death and the dying process. However, this line of thinking "tends to ignore that the speaker's acts arise and take shape in the context of jointly enacted and mutually recognized activities. Such acts as self-disclosure, information seeking, compliance gaining, and the like do not occur in conversational vacuum; they are enacted, recognized and responded to in the context of larger units of talk . . ." (Goldsmith & Baxter, 1996, p. 89).

Goldsmith and Baxter (1996) continue their discussion by suggesting that "small talk," has

> . . . been viewed as an instrument by which the individual reduces
> uncertainty in initial interaction, thereby providing the groundwork
> for the accomplishment of the relational goal of increased intimacy
> in the relationship. Recognition of the constitutive function of small

talk focuses instead on the ways in which relationships exist in small talk. When partners enact in small talk, that is the nature of their relationship; an ongoing pattern of conversations that are limited to small talk constitutes a particular kind of relationship between the parties, and they reproduce this relationship type every time they engage in small talk. In contrast, a relationship that includes frequent episodes of small talk as well as other kinds of talk is constituted differently and the nature and significance of small talk may be understood differently, as well" (p. 90).

The interactive process of small talk, introduced by Goldsmith and Baxter, provide a useful framework in which to place and understand the communicative acts of metaphors and euphemisms used by oncology healthcare professionals and patients in a different way then commonly perceived.

Often euphemisms and metaphors are part of "small talk" interactions. They are used to reduce anxiety or fears and establish rapport among individuals regarding particular events, such as end of life discussions. In an earlier passage we read how Marcy spoke of using metaphors in her frequent conversations with patients, to help reduce their fears about dying and establish a trusting rapport. Jeff, the social worker, also mentions how he told a metaphoric parable about God to convince a female cancer patient to take radiation treatment because she felt she could only be cured through an act of God. Sometimes these acts of communication may not be appropriate or simply ineffective, and another line of action is necessary (i.e., Jeff's patient did not go for radiation treatment). What is important to note is do the nurse, doctor, social worker, and patient agree upon that metaphors and euphemism are an integral part of their relationship or interpretive realities? If so, use of metaphors and euphemisms may not only represent the true nature of patient/caregiver relationships, but may also be *the* compassionate and sensitive thing to do at that moment or during changes in stages of illness.

In the end (no metaphor intended), the type of relationship that exists between the oncology healthcare professional and patient may primarily depend upon the symbolic use of metaphors and euphemisms.

CONCLUDING THOUGHTS

The emphasis throughout this last section has been to examine the meanings behind the death-related experiences, and associated acts by oncology healthcare professionals from the theoretical, qualitative perspective of symbolic interactionism.

Although the symbolic interactionism perspective was stressed, readers also became familiar with a rich variety of interpretive positions that lent themselves to the study of death and its' role in life. Whatever perspective is highlighted to better understand the area of death and human behavior, whether it is psychology, sociology, philosophy, or personal stories, they all give singular shape and meaning to the reality of it. All perspectives therefore are inherently limited because other views of reality are often omitted. The strength of theories thus lay with credible discussion and realistic applicability to people's unique daily circumstances.

The symbolic interactionist position has provided noted value and applicability for the study of death-related experiences among oncology healthcare professionals. Its focus on the individual and interpretive reality one attaches to self and others within real life contexts helps crystallize, through the use of language and other symbol systems, identity-formation, coping skills, communicative processes, and motives behind the person who chooses to face the likelihood of death and dying every day.

We have also seen in this section *how* individuals face the chaotic mix of death, dying, and daily life cannot be easily predicted. Often they are uniquely complicated and profound experiences. Perhaps, all anyone can do in the perplexing search for a meaningful life within the shadowy presence of death, is best articulated by Ernest Becker (1973):

> Who knows what form the forward momentum of life will take in the time ahead or what use it will make of our anguished searching. The most anyone can seem to do is fashion something—an object or ourselves—and drop it into the confusion, make an offering to it, so to speak, to the life force (p. 285).

What we do know is that such an offering is reserved only for the living.

Bibliography

Barnard, D. (1994, September). Closing plenary session. *The Tenth International Terminal Care Conference,* Montreal, Quebec.

Buckman, R. (1997). Communication in palliative care: A practice guide. *Palliative Medicine* (2nd Ed. Vol. 11:2), 141-156.

Buckman, R. (1989). *I don't know what to say: How to help and support someone who is dying.* New York: Vintage Books.

Becker, E. (1973). *The denial of death.* New York: The Free Press.

Berger, P. L., & Luckmann, T. (1966). *The social construction of reality.* New York: Anchor Press.

Blumer, H. (1969). *Symbolic interactionism: Perspective and method.* Englewood Cliffs, NJ: Prentice-Hall.

Charmaz, K. (1980). *The social reality of death; Death in contemporary America,* Reading, MA: Addison-Wesley.

Charon, J. M. (1998). *Symbolic interactionism: An introduction, an interpretation, an integration.* Upper Saddle River, NJ: Prentice-Hall.

Cooley, C. H. (1968). The social self: On the meanings of I. In: C. Gordon & K. J. Gergen (Eds.), *The self in social interactions (Vol. 1), Classic and contemporary perspectives* (pp. 87-91). New York: Wiley.

Corr, C. A. (1997, March). Death in modern society. *Palliative Medicine* (2nd Ed. Vol. 11:2), 31-40.

De Vries, R. G. (1981, June). Birth and death: Social construction at the poles of existence. *Social Forces, 59*:4, 1074-1093.

Duck, S., & Pond, K. (1989). Friends, Romans, countrymen, lend me your retrospective data: Rhetoric and reality in personal relationships. In C. Hendrick (Ed.), *Close relationships* (pp. 3-27). Newbury Park, CA: Sage.

Enright, D. J. (1983). *DEATH.* New York: Oxford University Press.

Fagermoen, S. M. (1997). Professional identity: Values embedded in meaningful nursing practice. *Journal of Advanced Nursing, 25,* 434-441.

Fife, B. L. (1994). The conceptualization of meaning in illness. *Social Science and Medicine, 38*:2, 309-316.

Goffman, E. (1959a). *The presentation of self in everyday life.* New York: Doubleday.

Goffman, E. (1959b). On face-work: An analysis of ritual elements in social interaction. In: *Interaction ritual* (pp. 5-45). Garden City, NY: Anchor Books.

Goldsmith, D. J., & Baxter, L. A. (1996, September). Constituting relationships in talk: A taxonomy of speech events in social and personal relationships. *Human Communication Research, 23*:1, 87-114.

Gergen, K. J. (1985). Social constructionist inquiry: Context and implications. In: K. J. Gergen & K. E. Danz (Eds.), *The social construction of the person* (pp. 11-17). New York: Springer-Verlag.

Gudykunst, W. B., & Bradford, H. J. (1994). Strategies for effective communication and adaptation in intergroup context. In: J. A. Daley & J. M. Wieman (Eds.), *Strategic interpersonal communication* (pp. 225-272). Hillsdale, NJ: Lawrence Erlbaum Associates, Inc.

Kübler-Ross, E. (1969). *On death and dying.* New York: Collier Books, Macmillan.

Marguis, S. (1993). Death of the nursed: Burnout of the provider. *Omega, 27*:1, 17-33.

McCormick, T. R., & Conley, B. J. (1993). Patients' perspective on dying and on the care of dying patients. In: Caring for patients the end of life [Special Issue]. *Western Journal of Medicine, 163,* 236-243.

Nuland, S. B. (1993). *HOW WE DIE: Reflections on life's final chapter.* New York: Vintage Books.

Novack, D., & Suchman, A. L. (1997). Calibrating the physician: Personal awareness and effective patient care. *Journal of the American Medical Association, 278*:6, 502-509.

Pearce, W. B. (1976). The coordinated management of meaning: A rules-based theory of interpersonal communication. In: G. R. Miller (Ed.), *Explorations in Interpersonal Communication,* London: Sage.

Peters, J. D. (1999). Introduction: The problem of communication. In: *Speaking into the air: A history of the idea of communication* (pp. 1-31). Chicago: University of Chicago Press.

Schlenker, B. R. (1986). Self identification. In: R. F. Baumeister (Ed.), *Public self and private self* (pp. 21-62). New York: Springer-Verlag.

Schott, S. (1979). Emotion and social life: A symbolic interactionist analysis. *American Journal of Sociology, 84*: 317-334.

Sexton, J. P. (1997). Death and dying: Metaphor and morality. *Etc. Cetera,* 223-245.

Simonton, O. C., Simonton, S.-M., & Creighton, J. L. (1978). *Getting well again.* New York: Bantam Books.

Sudrow, D. (1967). *Passing on: The social organization of dying.* Englewood Cliffs: Prentice-Hall.

Surbone, A. (1997). Information, truth and communication. In: A Surbone & M. Switter (Eds.), *Annals of the New York Academy of Science: Communication with Cancer Patients, 809,* 7-16.

Trenholm, S., & Jensen, A. (2000). *Interpersonal communication* (6th ed.). Belmont, CA: Wadsworth.

Vachon, M. S. (1997). The stress of professional caregivers. *Palliative Medicine* (2nd ed. Vol. 11:2), 919-929.

Van Servellen, G. (1997). *Communication skills for the healthcare professional: Concepts and techniques.* Gaithersburg, MD: Aspen.

Index